SPEAKING FOR THE ENSLAVED

HERITAGE, TOURISM, AND COMMUNITY

Series Editor: Helaine Silverman
University of Illinois at Urbana-Champaign

Heritage, Tourism, and Community is an innovative new book series that seeks to address these interconnected issues from multidisciplinary and interdisciplinary perspectives. Manuscripts are sought that address heritage and tourism and their relationships to local community, economic development, regional ecology, heritage conservation and preservation, and related indigenous, regional, and national political and cultural issues. Manuscripts, proposals, and letters of inquiry should be submitted to *helaine@uiuc.edu*.

Speaking for the Enslaved: Heritage Interpretation at Antebellum Plantation Sites, *Antoinette T. Jackson*

Heritage That Hurts: Tourists in the Memoryscapes of September 11, *Joy Sather-Wagstaff*

Inconvenient Heritage: Erasure and Global Tourism in Luang Prabang, *Lynne Dearborn and John C. Stallmeyer*

Coach Fellas: Heritage and Tourism in Ireland, *Kelli Ann Costa*

The Tourists Gaze, The Cretans Glance: Archaeology and Tourism on a Greek Island, *Philip Duke*

SPEAKING FOR THE ENSLAVED

Heritage Interpretation at Antebellum Plantation Sites

Antoinette T. Jackson

Walnut Creek, California

LEFT COAST PRESS, INC.
1630 North Main Street, #400
Walnut Creek, CA 94596
http://www.LCoastPress.com

ISBN 978-1-59874-548-1 hardback
ISBN 978-1-59874-549-8 paperback
ISBN 978-1-59874-550-4 institutional eBook
ISBN 978-1-61132-618-5 consumer eBook

Library of Congress Cataloging-in-Publication Data:

Jackson, Antoinette T.
Speaking for the enslaved : heritage interpretation at antebellum plantation sites / Antoinette T. Jackson.
    p. cm. — (Heritage, tourism, and community)
Includes bibliographical references and index.
ISBN 978-1-59874-548-1 (hbk. : alk. paper) — ISBN 978-1-59874-549-8 (pbk. : alk. paper) — ISBN 978-1-59874-550-4 (institutional ebook) — ISBN 978-1-61132-618-5 (consumer ebook)
1. Historic sites—Interpretive programs—Southern States. 2. Plantations—Southern States. 3. African Americans—Southern States—Social life and customs. 4. Plantation life—Southern States—History. 5. Community life—Southern States—History. 6. Material culture—Southern States—History. 7. Southern States—Antiquities. 8. Public history—Social aspects—Southern States. 9. Memory—Social aspects—Southern States. 10. Southern States—Cultural policy. I. Title.
    F210.J33 2012
    975—dc23
                                        2012000882

Printed in the United States of America

♾ ™ The paper used in this publication meets the minimum requirements of American National Standard for Information Sciences—Permanence of Paper for Printed Library Materials, ANSI/NISO Z39.48–1992.

CONTENTS

For my ancestors

For making a way

ILLUSTRATIONS AND TABLES

Foreword

by Paul A. Shackel

The interpretation and inclusion of subaltern groups into the national public memory is often contested, and Antoinette Jackson in her finely crafted book, *Speaking for the Enslaved: Heritage Interpretation in Antebellum Plantation Sites*, provides several case studies dealing with African-American representation in the southeastern United States. All too often narratives create simple dichotomies of the past that separate ethnic groups into distinctive, simple categories. For African Americans in the southeast, these categories at plantation sites usually include "slaves" in the antebellum era and "sharecroppers" in the postbellum era. Public tours and the literature distributed to visitors at these plantations usually focus on the life and struggles of the plantation owners, and any interpretations of African Americans usually receive only generic references to slavery. Jackson's work challenges these traditional narratives.

By examining the heritage preservation and interpretation at several nationally known sites, Jackson shows that the past is often much more complicated than what is presented to the public. Such places as Friendfield, Jehossee Island, and Snee Farm plantations in South Carolina, and Kingsley Plantation in Florida, are contested grounds where forgotten narratives are beginning to help to create a more inclusive past and present. Jackson uses these narratives from the descendant community to complicate the stories of the past in order to create a more inclusive heritage. From collected oral histories from African-American descendants of Jehossee Island, now part of a National Wildlife Refuge in South Carolina, she counters the dominant narrative of the black community—slaves in the antebellum era and sharecroppers in the postbellum era. The enslaved Africans were responsible for many aspects of rice production, including as field hands, engineers, sailors, cooks, midwives, teachers, and artisans. The omission of this more textured story is, I believe, a continuation of the racism that continues to exist today—a racism that is not necessarily overt but rather covert. It is a racism by omission.

Jackson notes that anthropologists are calling for the systematic unveiling and recovery of subjugated knowledges, which is an important and necessary step in any social science. However, I believe that another major issues is this: Who is subjugating the knowledge and why? The exclusion of people and their misrepresentation is a political act, and it is a process that helped to reinforce a narrative that allowed for a white hegemony in the present.

Changing the narrative is often a result of a significant national grass roots effort. In some instances, the change is truly political. In this book, Jackson notes that some places, such as the Charles Pinckney house, a National Park Service site, have broadened the narrative's interpretation not only to commemorate a noted drafter of the U.S. Constitution and a fierce proponent of slavery but also to include the many unknown Africans who worked on and around the plantation house. This more inclusive approach developed at the turn of this century, and it is a product of the political pressure applied by Congressman Jesse Jackson, Jr. In 1998, Congressman Jackson encouraged the National Park Service to increase African-American representation at national parks. As a result, park managers held a conference titled "Holding the High Ground." The document from the meeting explains that the National Park Service was telling the story at these places that has traditionally been biased racially and socioeconomically, since it told the story of only the literate and enfranchised. A number of national parks have addressed this issue of representation and enslavement, and the stories of African Americans are now part of many more national parks. However, even as we move into the second decade of the twenty-first century, not all parks have created more inclusive narratives that allow all people as part of our national public memory.

Examining the public interpretation at these nationally significant sites, Antoinette Jackson shows how heritage preservation professionals and local and descendant communities often have different perspectives and stories at these places. In fact, Jackson states that it is imperative that descendant knowledge be sought and included as part of the management, interpretation, and preservation process of these nationally significant sites.

The use of descendant knowledge and its political force at historic sites has been shown to be rather profitable in other research programs. For instance, in the archaeology project at New Philadelphia in west central Illinois, a multiracial town established on the Illinois frontier in 1836, the inclusion of the descendant community expanded the narrative to develop a more inclusive message about the place, thereby expanding the local support for this heritage project. In Philadelphia, the construction of the Liberty Bell Center in 2003 led to a protest of 500 people asking that the enslaved be remembered with the construction of a memorial. Protesters also demanded that the rest of the President's House site be excavated to reveal and interpret the story of the President's House, which included the life of the enslaved African Americans. As a consequence, the National Park Service was asked by the Pennsylvania State Legislature and the Philadelphia City Council to develop a design that would commemorate the residents and the enslaved African Americans. In another example, in 1991, construction began for a new federal office building in Lower Manhattan sponsored by the General Services Administration (GSA). Between the summers of 1991 and 1992, over 400 human burials were recovered at the construction site at a place known as the Negro Burial Grounds. Congress stepped in and ended the excavations. Mayor Dinkins provided support, and many community organizations and clergy rallied behind the preservation of the remaining parts of the burial ground. The GSA redesigned the office building to allow for the preservation of the remaining parts of the cemetery and to create a memorial plaza. There are examples of hard-fought cases to extend the narrative to include the African-American experience.

Antoinette Jackson's book is about extending and complicating the history of African Americans and providing a new and more inclusive perspective for our national public memory. *Speaking for the Enslaved: Heritage Interpretation in Antebellum Plantation Sites* lays a foundation to challenge the dominant narrative, and it shows how the descendant community can add a more inclusive and textured story about the past.

Preface

First Lady Michelle Obama's connection to a former antebellum plantation site in the United States highlights the central theme of this book—privileging descendant voices and telling a bigger story about America's history and heritage. Friendfield Plantation, located in Georgetown, South Carolina, was the site of a thriving rice plantation in the mid-1800s. Today it is a privately owned estate that is listed on the National Register of Historic Places in America. Friendfield has gained national attention primarily because Mrs. Obama's family lineage has been traced to enslaved African ancestors who lived and worked at the site. In describing her recently acquired knowledge of her family's roots and the significance of that information today, Michelle Obama, in an interview with the *Washington Post* in October of 2008, said: "It's good to be a part of playing out history in this way. It could be anybody. But it's us, it's our family, it's that story that's going to play a part in telling a bigger story" (Murray 2008:C01). The bigger story is America's story as expressed by descendants of enslaved Africans and others associated with antebellum plantation sites.

Colonial and antebellum accounts of plantation life typically characterize persons of African descent solely as slaves. I argue that to reduce discussion of Africans in plantation spaces to slave life portraits is to perpetuate a narrow vision of American history. In this work, I place emphasis on linking the past to the present through descendant voices— showing that although Africans were restricted by their enslavement, they cannot be defined universally and completely within this context. Rather, they developed ways of living in antebellum plantation spaces and positioned their communities and families for the future. I interpret and profile plantations as dynamic spaces of intricate and intimately connected communities of people actively engaged in developing strategies for living and surviving.

Today many of these former antebellum plantation sites are located within federally designated National Heritage Areas. Such areas are recognized as containing material, cultural, and historical resources that are to be preserved and interpreted for future generations. Critiquing how heritage is preserved, managed, and interpreted in former antebellum plantation spaces is an important aspect of the heritage resource management process—particularly in the case of national historic sites and federally designated national heritage areas.

As a member of the Gullah/Geechee National Heritage Corridor Commission and an academically trained and employed cultural anthropologist of African descent, I am interested in how multiple and sometimes conflicting roles and responsibilities of designated cultural resource experts engaged in this effort—from local community experts, to credentialed academics, to state appointed preservation officials to the National Park Service (NPS)—affect the completion of mandated goals and objectives in areas of heritage preservation, interpretation, and tourism. I am also interested in understanding my own roots more holistically in the context of the transatlantic slave trade and U.S. American history.

Many people have posed the question: Why go back to the plantation? Why bother reconstructing a negative time in American history? I understand their sentiment and skepticism. Even now, just recalling the short version of what I so meticulously learned is unsettling—enslaved African people portrayed solely as victims and forced to labor on demand. In school I remember stifling feelings of embarrassment behind a mask of indifference when the subject of slavery was discussed. I saw no use in looking back at that period in history. After all, what could be learned from people in such a state?

The answer lies in analyzing how people encounter plantations and interact within plantations spaces in the contemporary present. This book expands ways thinking about antebellum plantation sites and enslaved African people and their descendants to include more nuanced perspectives concerning plantation life and methodological tools and strategies for addressing issues of heritage preservation, interpretation, and tourism more critically. Chapters 1 and 2 focus on assessing the past. Specifically, Chapter 1 provides an introduction to heritage in context to other ways of knowing the past. Additionally, issues of identity and representation as they pertain to former antebellum plantations designated as public historic sites and located within federally designated National Heritage Areas in the United States are addressed. Such sites have often been marked/marketed primarily from the perspective of white male plantation-owning elite. They provide limited interpretations that reflect critically on the lives of enslaved Africans, their descendants, and others directly affected by representations that fix people in static categories (that is, slave, sharecropper, wage worker) with adverse implications in terms of power and import in the present.

Chapter 2 examines issues in heritage tourism, management, and preservation, particularly focusing on multistakeholder and multiuse expectations for heritage resources/assets encountered in pursuit of large-scale public heritage initiatives on a community level. There are tensions, for example, associated with managing heritage as an asset for preservation and heritage as a product for consumption. I introduce concepts and lessons shared by McKercher and du Cros (2002), resulting from their observations and collaboration as heritage professionals representing tourism and cultural heritage management, respectively. Their work offers multiple ways of thinking about heritage assets/products and their potential use across stakeholder groups, as well as offering ways of circumventing problems encountered. For example, the National Register of Historic Places, State Historical Markers, surveys of historic materials through Historic American Buildings Survey (HABS) and Historic American Engineering Record (HAER) programs, and others sources engaged in preservation of historic sites, buildings, and objects of national importance typically managed by the State Historic Preservation Office (SHPO) located in states throughout the country are used in different ways by stakeholders interested in heritage tourism and stakeholders interested in heritage resource management. Additionally, I introduce a federally designated National Heritage Area, the Gullah/Geechee Cultural Heritage Corridor, because it contains information of significance with respect to American history in general, as well as insight into how living communities address issues of cultural/heritage management. Chapter 2 makes a case for the importance of recognizing varied use possibilities for heritage assets and articulating these expectations during the planning phase as part of the partnership agreement and implementation strategy for those engaged in managing heritage initiatives.

I conclude discussions initiated in Chapters 1 and 2 by formally proposing that descendant knowledge be sought and included as part of the heritage tourism, management, and preservation process. In the case of interpretations of antebellum plantation sites as those presented in this work, descendant knowledge is a means of broadening ways of thinking about Africans in plantation spaces beyond fixed notions of laboring roles and social and geographic place expectations.

Chapters 3, 4, 5, and 6 focus on *Telling a Bigger Story*. In these chapters, I go beyond benign stories of plantation life often presented to visitors in guided tours and interpretative presentations about former antebellum plantation sites and construct a bigger more critically interpretive story about U.S. American history and heritage. These chapters recast the history of slavery and the construction of community in America by consciously soliciting and using descendant voices to develop a rubric of knowledge privileging the complex and often underrepresented role played by majority African communities in former antebellum plantation spaces. Descendants shed light on broader dynamics for characterizing plantations. I propose that telling a bigger story includes using descendant voices and descendant knowledge to instruct the development of tools and processes of analyzes that sidesteps the solidifying effect of rigid categorization systems. Stories about Friendfield, Jehossee Island, and Snee Farm plantations in South Carolina, and Kingsley Plantation in Florida, presented in these chapters all draw on descendant knowledge in distinctly instructive ways.

I begin with Friendfield Plantation and Michelle Obama's very American story in Chapter 3. A concern throughout is—what is the significance of Friendfield Plantation in terms of descendants of enslaved Africans, and what does it mean today in terms of the history and heritage of America? Chapter 4 informs the process of recovering knowledge that has been subjugated in order to redress silences about Africans, Europeans, and the production of rice on a former antebellum plantation site in the United States. On Jehossee Island, now part of the ACE Basin National Wildlife Refuge in South Carolina, enslaved African people were responsible for all aspects of commercial rice production—from field hands, to engineers, to sailors, to cooks, midwives, teachers, and artisans. Yet this is not the story that tourist brochures tell. Chapter 5 addresses the effect of systems of categorization on identity and representation. Emphasis is placed on critically analyzing how fixed and universally applied systems of categorization with respect to laboring roles of enslaved Africans and their descendants in former antebellum plantation spaces in Mount Pleasant, South Carolina, have acted to mask a diversity of skills, experiences, responsibilities, and expertise across generations. For example, "Tell them we were never sharecroppers" was the phrase I heard when interviewing descendants of enslaved Africans that had previously lived and worked on Snee Farm and Boone Hall plantations in Mount Pleasant—places of enslavement for their ancestors. However, this descriptive, although widely presented in tourist brochures, universally denoted as classifying the laboring history for an entire community or group of people, is applied inaccurately. I interviewed painters, cooks, artists, deacons, longshoremen, Park Rangers, fishermen, basketmakers, gardeners, and business owners—all descendants of enslaved Africans who did not agree with fixed representations and universal categorization of their or their ancestors' labor. Analysis of oral history data collected as part of my study shows that enslaved Africans and their descendants do not universally fit into any one labor/laboring category. Chapter 6 examines the Kingsley Plantation and community from a diasporic perspective and introduces ways of interpreting antebellum plantations beyond fixed notions of social and geographic place. Specifically, the life and business activities of Zephaniah Kingsley, Jr., born in Bristol, England in 1765, and Anta Majigeen Ndiaye (Anna Kingsley), born in Senegal, West Africa in 1793, tell an important story. Kingsley purchased and fathered children with Anna and later freed her and established households and businesses with her in Florida and Haiti. Their lives underscore the need for analyzing the fluidity of roles, relationships, and associations with places people call home today in the context of the transatlantic slave trade. In other words, the Kingsleys are a multiracial, multinational family. And stories of descendants, such as Mr. Manuel Lebrón's account of his participation in the annual Kingsley Heritage celebration held at the Kingsley Plantation site, provide expanded representations of place that go beyond the interpretive boundaries delineated by the National Park Service. Descendants can provide insight into the transition and movement of African descendant people within and outside antebellum plantation landscapes.

Throughout the book, I focus on several key questions: (1) In which ways does knowledge shared by enslaved Africans and their descendants living in, or associated with, plantation spaces through stories, rituals, traditions, and memories help to inform interpretation of U.S. plantation sites in the contemporary present? (2) What tools, questions, and methods can be used to research and profile people and communities whose stories have gone untold or have been relegated to the margins of mainstream public discourse of American history? More specifically, how do the ways in which African and African-American history and heritage are represented (or not) at National Heritage sites and other public sites deemed to be of historical significance inform our knowledge of U.S. history and culture? (3) What role can heritage and heritage resource management practices play in expanding public understanding of antebellum and postbellum plantations as communities and sites of knowledge through incorporation of descendant voices?

Although many of these questions are currently being debated in the public forum (Fennell 2010; Orser 2007; Ruffins 2006; Shackel 2003, 2011), this book approaches such questions from a cultural anthropology perspective aimed at a multidisciplinary population of scholars and students as well as anyone interested in critically engaging the politics of identity and representation. This profile and analysis of former antebellum plantation communities marks distinct yet interconnected ways of interpreting plantation spaces in the contemporary present. In chapters that follow, theories and methods of archaeology of the contemporary present (Buchli and Lucas 2001), as well as theories and methods of cultural anthropology, including the ethnographic method—aimed at knowing and interpreting the present—are brought into bold relief. Developing interpretations from this intersection of approaches to knowing equips future generations with dynamic and expanded ways of talking about history. In this case, U.S. American history and heritage as understood from the perspective of enslaved Africans and their descendants contemporarily as an active act of interpretation/re-interpretation.

I have been consumed with the topic of heritage for a long time. I approach the topic from the perspective of the global legacy of the transatlantic slave trade. My journey to explore heritage on local and specific levels in communities throughout the United States influenced by this reality has been and continues to be a challenging one. I welcome your participation in this conversation.

An explanation of the book's title is appropriate. As the author of this work, I am not speaking for the enslaved. Rather, I am introducing descendant voices, observations, interpretations, and critiques, as well as other intangible and tangible resources, as sites/sources of knowledge providing new ways of speaking out loud about issues of import to interpreting antebellum plantation spaces and the lives of enslaved Africans and their descendants.

ACKNOWLEDGMENTS

This book has been a long time in the making, and I have gone through many stages of my life's journey in the pursuit of getting to this point. I was first called to action in the service of this book in 1996 on a trip to Egypt by way of relationships I had established with the Gullah Geechee community in South Carolina. I have been in the process of writing it ever since. Along the way, I have changed careers from a business professional in the telecommunications industry working for AT&T/Lucent Technologies to an academic—completing my Ph.D. in 2004 and becoming a tenured Associate Professor of Anthropology at the University of South Florida in 2011, and now author of this book. The acknowledgments that follow reflect the various stages of my journey and the deeply meaningful encounters, relationships, and influences along the way. I have been most abundantly blessed and am thankful for each and every person who has entered my life when he or she did, because I have learned so much. Even though I cannot name everyone, please accept my sincere gratitude. However, I do want to give special mention to my family—my parents, Jesse and Mercedes Jackson, my brother Gregory E. Jackson, and my sisters, Yolanda N. Jackson and Jacqueline A. Jackson—for their unconditional love and constant encouragement. Also special thanks to members of my dissertation Committee at the University of Florida—Dr. John Moore, Chair, Dr. Allan F. Burns, Dr. Kesha Fikes, and Dr. Hugh Popenoe—and everyone else who supported and encouraged me in this stage of my development.

This book is based on research conducted under National Park Service (NPS) contract No. P5440990154, "Ethnographic and Ethnohistorical Report on Snee Farm, Charles Pinckney National Historic Site" and research conducted under NPS contract No. Q5038000491, "Ethnohistorical Study of Kingsley Plantation Community." I owe particular acknowledgment to those persons in the community of Mount Pleasant whom I interviewed in the summer of 2000 and whose words and teachings appear in this text, such as Ms. Martha (Mattie) Gaillard (now deceased), Reverend Harry Palmer, and members of the Brown family.

I would like to extend specific project acknowledgments and a thank you to the following persons for their interest in and support of the Kingsley Plantation project: Marsha Dean Phelts for research leads and her wealth of knowledge on the history of Jacksonville's African-American community; Dr. Allan F. Burns, for his interest, insight, support, and encouragement; Dr. Anthony Paredes for his attention to detail, constructive feedback on submitted materials, and consistent and positive support; Barbara Goodman (NPS Superintendent of Fort Caroline National Memorial and Timucuan Ecological and Historic Preserve) and John Whitehurst (Cultural Resource Manager, NPS Timucuan Ecological and Historic Preserve) for their support and the support of their staff; Paul Ghioto (NPS Timucuan Preserve) for being an excellent St. Johns River boat pilot and informative guide; Lydia Stewart (LaVilla Museum Administrator) for great community contacts and use of LaVilla Museum office facilities; Bruce Chappell (archivist/manuscripts University of Florida–Special Collections) and Jim Cussack (curator, Florida History–University of Florida Special Collections) for their archival support and in-depth knowledge of Florida history data sources; Charles Tingley (Library Manager) and G. Leslie Wilson (Assistant Library Manager) at the St. Augustine Historical Society for their knowledge, insight, and resource and reference leads; Eileen Brady (Librarian, Special Collections Dept., University of North Florida Library, Eartha M. M. White Collection) for her time, as well as her respect for and thorough knowledge of Eartha White's life and history; J. N. Eaton and E. Murrell Dawson (Florida A&M Black Archives Research Center and Museum) for their knowledge of and access to files and data on black life in Florida pre- and post-Civil War period; Kay Tullis (Jacksonville Historical Society) for access to Kingsley Plantation files and information; Glenn Emery (Sr. Librarian Florida Collection, Jacksonville Public Library); Durkeeville Historical Center; Florida State Archives–Archives and Records Management team; Lydia Wooden and Charlotte Stewart for sharing information and photos about their family and early Jacksonville history; Peter House and family for their support and knowledge of Arlington/Clifton community of Jacksonville; Dr. Martha Ellen Davis and her informant Crucito Medina Kingsley Eleibo of the Dominican Republic, for access to their files and research data on Zephaniah Kingsley's Dominican Republic connections; my Kingsley project research team, Terry Weik, Katisha Greer, Jodi Skipper, Flemming Daugaard, Ermitte St. Jacques, Jennifer Hale-Gallardo, and Maxine Downs. Big thanks to Yolanda N. Jackson (Nevada Graphics) for her patience and encouragement throughout the process. I would also like to extend a special acknowledgment to those persons who agreed to be interviewed or videotaped for the Kingsley Plantation project in 1998 and 2001, especially those whose words and insights appear in this text, such as Dr. Johnnetta B. Cole and Mr. Manuel Lebrón. I would like to extend an additional thank you to Mr. Lebrón for agreeing to let me interview him in November 2010 and for updating me on his and his family's lives.

As I enter the final stages of producing this work and once again reflect on the journey, I am thankful for the spiritual and educational guidance I received from the Temple of the African Community (TACC) in Chicago, the knowledge, friendship, and love I received from Gullah Geechee people and the Gullah/Geechee Cultural Heritage Corridor Commission, the financial support, mentorship and fellowship I received as a FEF McKnight Fellow, as well as the support and encouragement of students and colleagues at the University of South Florida. I am grateful and indebted to Rachel Breunlin, Dana-Ain Davis, Susan Fitzpatrick-Behrens, Rod Dixon, Jennifer Hale-Gallardo, Mari Gillogly, Helen Regis, Mayumi Shimose, Daryl Thompson, and Kim Vaz, as well as, the editor of this book series, Helaine Silverman, and publisher of Left Coast Press, Inc., Mitch Allen, and many other reviewers of this book throughout its various stages of creation and production for encouragement, critique, editing support, and constructive and transformative suggestions, feedback, and most of all for an unwavering belief in me and the importance of getting the project done. It is done. The ancestors are satisfied—*Ashé*.

Antoinette T. Jackson
May, 2012

Chapter 1

HISTORY, HERITAGE, MEMORY, PLACE

Heritage is not our sole link with the past. History, tradition, memory, myth, and memoir variously join us with what has passed, with fore-bears, with our earlier selves. Yet the lure of heritage now outpaces other modes of retrieval.

—David Lowenthal (1996:3), *Possessed by the Past*

That heritage can be sustained only by a living community becomes an accepted tenet. To sustain a legacy of stones, those who dwell among them also need stewardship.

—David Lowenthal (1996:21), *Possessed by the Past*

HERITAGE

Heritage is being discussed everywhere it seems, and typically with passion. Solidly part of the public domain of inquiry, it is a subject that most people have an intimate relationship with—academics, public officials, dignitaries, elders, and youth alike. The journey to know our heritage represents a profound desire to see ourselves in the continuum of history on a family, community, national, or global level. It is a quest to know more about ourselves and to share that knowledge with others through a variety of means. Questions such as these are common: Who am I? What stories, memories, and what traditions are important to my family and within my community? Each generation asks how these stories are reflected in the public record and by whose authority.

But what is heritage exactly? How is it defined, expressed, and shared? Can my desire to express my heritage coexist with your right to express yours? What happens when multiple expressions and ways of expressing heritage collide in public forums or, perhaps even more challenging, fail to even exist in public venues and forums?

There are numerous definitions of heritage (Chambers 2006; Herbert 1985; Howard 2003; Karp, Kreamer, and Lavine 1992; Lowenthal 1985, 1996). For example, in his book *Possessed by the Past* David Lowenthal (1996) offers several ways of thinking about heritage. First, he defines the difference between history and heritage, which he claims is a vital distinction—"History explores and explains pasts grown ever more opaque over time; heritage clarifies pasts so as to infuse them with present purposes" (Lowenthal 1996:xi). Then, in the passage that I use to open this chapter, Lowenthal goes on to place heritage in the context of other ways of knowing and experiencing the past, an important organizing perspective. Fath Davis Ruffins (1992) critically elaborates on ways of knowing and interpreting the past. She examines the very idea of "the past" in the context of modes of interpretation—history, memory, and mythos—specifically applying her analysis to African-American preservation efforts. She writes: "One way to think about the past as being different from history is to see historical interpretation as a snapshot of the past" (Ruffins 1992:509). Figure 1.1 graphically illustrates the positioning of heritage in the context of other ways of knowing the past as elaborated on by Lowenthal (1996) and Ruffins (1992).

Building on definitions outlined by Ruffins (1992) and Lowenthal (1996), I think it is important to critique what is meant by the past and

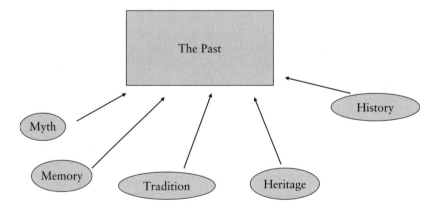

Links to the Pasts. Ways of engaging with the past.

Figure 1.1 Engaging the past (courtesy of author)

to consider the distinction between history and heritage. Ruffins states that "historical interpretation of the past is made out of selections of the past by people in the present in order to help them [to] understand both the past and the present" (1992:510). I define history as a story about the past—one of many that could be told at any given moment. The skill of the history maker is determined by the evidence used to tell the story as judged by the stakeholders that sanction its production. And history, as Michel-Rolph Trouillot (1995) would have us note, is not only what happened but also what is said to have happened. The power is in the production and reproduction of the story in the present and the story's relevance to those affected.

I define *heritage* as anything a community, a nation, a stakeholder, or a family wants to save, make active, and continue in the present. Heritage is one way of engaging in or assessing the past (Figure 1.1). It is our living connection to history in the present moment—a connection that can be expressed in variety of ways, such as through rituals, traditions, stories, songs, memories, and myths. Heritage is both tangible (material cultural remains such as buildings, monuments, tombs, and bridges) and intangible (such as folkways, kinship, language, music, laboring practices, and artisan skills). Although more emphasis has been placed on preserving tangible aspects of heritage and of the past, there is increasing recognition of the importance of preservation of intangible cultural heritage as an important link to the past, particularly seen in the construction of internationally sanctioned conventions or guidelines directed at this goal. In 2003, for example, UNESCO (United Nations Educational, Scientific, and Cultural Organization) proposed *Conventions for the Safeguarding of Intangible Cultural Heritage* (UNESCO 2003). Like the 1972 UNESCO *Convention Concerning the Protection of World Cultural and Natural Heritage* (1972), it deals with cultural heritage and its protection. However, as of the printing of this book, the 2003 Convention is still awaiting ratification by a significant body of UNESCO member states, including the United States.

Erve Chambers (2006) defines two categories of heritage—public and private (personal). Private heritage is described as tangible and intangible items or things that individuals inherit and pass down to later generations. It consists of information expressed through daily routines and actions, which are not necessarily sanctioned by an official authority (for example, the National Park Service). Essentially it is the way things are done in your family, your organization, or your neighborhood, which is passed on to the next generation or group of participants through symbols, rituals, and language, for example. Public heritage is the sharing and transmission of recorded information about things, such as a place, an event, or a person that we may have no direct experience with knowing. It is typically information presented and shared by "official" or sanctioned keepers of history, such as museums, libraries, and historical societies and historical preservation boards in the form of written text, graphics, pictures, selected artifacts, and designated structures. By collecting ethnographic and ethnohistorical data (for example, oral histories, community maps, housing statistics, cemetery data, civic records, census data) across diverse segments of families, communities, and neighborhoods, covering a range of periods of time, one sees a public profile of the history and heritage of a community, of a nation (for example, the United States), emerge that is more representative of the breadth and depth of experiences and memories of all people that call that place home.

Finally, we must recognize the distinction between heritage as a cultural asset for conservation and preservation, such as viewed by groups focused on cultural heritage management, and the use of heritage as a product or commodity for consumption and sale from a business perspective, such as the case in heritage tourism. It is a distinction that is critically engaged in the book *Cultural Tourism* by McKercher and du Cros (2002). Specifically, they underscore the need for groups invested in heritage from either perspective—conservation or consumption—to work in partnership or at least to strive to communicate more effectively during the planning and implementation phases of heritage projects in communities in which they work.

In all cases, heritage involves the construction of a story about the past that affects the present. Slavery, for example, plays a central role in the history and heritage of the United States. However, this is an underrepresented story when it comes to the construction of national heritage. In her article *Tourism and National Heritage (U.S.)* Allison Carter outlines links between national heritage, race, and place in terms of African-American communities and history. She writes: "Hence from its beginnings slavery, race, and place are essential components of any depiction of national heritage in the United States and as such become sites of contested meanings. African-American heritage tourism forces revisiting of conflicting discourses about the meaning of African-American experience in U.S. history, as well as the meaning of U.S. history itself" (Carter 2008:134).

RESEARCHING PLANTATIONS AND POSTBELLUM PLANTATION COMMUNITIES

A large body of scholarly work has been published on the transatlantic slave trade, plantation life, and slavery in the Americas, primarily by historians (Berlin 1998; Blassingame 1979 [1972]; Burton

1985; Eltis, Lewis, and Sokoloff 2004; Genovese 1976 [1974]; Morgan 1998; Phillips 1946 [1929]; Rawick 1972; Ruffins 2006; White 1985; Wood 1974). Historical archaeologists have also contributed to scholarship on plantations, in many cases linking African agency to the material record (Davidson 2008; Epperson 1999; Fairbanks 1974; Ferguson 1992; Leone and Potter 1988; McDavid 2007; Orser 1998, 2004, 2007; Shackel, Mullins, and Warner 1998; Singleton 1985, 1999, 2000; Vlach 1993; Wilkie 2000).[1] However, culturally oriented anthropological studies focused on African lifeways in antebellum and postbellum communities in the southeast region of the United States have been undertaken by a small group of scholars (Guthrie 1996; Jackson 2004; Jones-Jackson 1987; Mitchell 1999).

This analysis compels an expansion of the list of possible sources of information about plantations and slavery to include not only measurable facts that can be retrieved/excavated and interpreted but also less easily measurable sources of information—at least from a positivist perspective—for developing explanations. For example, oral history and ethnographic interview data can bring to light what Cooper, Holt, and Scott in *Beyond Slavery* characterize as the "messy, contradictory worlds that slaves and slaveowners created" (2000:7).

I draw on research I conducted in postbellum plantation communities in the U.S. South.[2] These communities challenge assumptions about American history and heritage constructed in the context of the transatlantic slave trade. By giving primacy to knowledge shared by enslaved Africans through their descendants, I document how Africans and people of African descent (identified as "black") developed ways of living in antebellum plantation spaces and created a future for their communities and families. Integrating archival data collection with qualitative research methods—such as ethnography, ethnographic interview, oral history, and participant observation—my research proposes that Africans in America engaged in various processes of culture and identity formation (including heritage preservation) through everyday acts of living—working, establishing families, raising children, caring for elders, and growing, harvesting, cooking and sharing food.[3] At the same time, they actively used resources, generated knowledge systems, developed communities, and exhibited behavior aimed at foiling, countering, and navigating within a Eurocentric system of power and control designed to limit their autonomy (Davis 1983 [1981]; Gutman 1976; Jackson 2004, 2009).

Interpreting the history and heritage of African communities in plantation spaces through perspectives shared by descendants—through their stories, expressions, critiques, and lived experiences—conveys what is best described by Patricia Hill Collins as an "outsider within" approach to knowing (Collins 1991:11). Participating in day-to-day activities seemingly unrelated to the transatlantic slave trade, descendants of enslaved Africans today and others (including descendants of plantation owners) often embody deeper, more complex meanings and associations with former antebellum plantation sites. Their knowledge, which has often been subjugated (Collins 1991; Foucault 1980 [1972]), is an important addition to the scholarly discourse and will help to reinterpret the practice of slavery in America in new, more complex ways. When scholars make these bodies of knowledge visible in the public record, their ways of knowing and thinking about African communities in plantation spaces are expanded. Anthropologists Ira E. Harrison and Faye V. Harrison call the systematic unveiling and recovery of subjugated knowledges a critical aspect of any transformative anthropological project, especially with respect to African Americans (1999). By offering a link to enslaved ancestors through intergenerational conversations—communication and direct engagement with parents, grandparents, and great grandparents—their stories are a means of speaking for the enslaved and providing a more nuanced interpretation of U.S. American history.

SLAVERY AND THE RACIAL CONSTRUCTION OF PUBLIC MEMORY

New voices have emerged to debate the proper place of slavery in the larger history of the United States. New institutions devoted to slavery as a subject will have to place themselves definitively within this contentious environment so as to garner financial and other forms of public support. In that complex process, a new synthesis may appear that honors both the suffering of the enslaved and their contributions to American society.
—Fath Davis Ruffins (2006:426–27), *Revisiting the Old Plantation: Reparations, Reconciliation, and Museumizing American Slavery*

When the U.S. Constitution was drafted and signed at the Constitutional Convention in Philadelphia in 1787 by fifty-five delegates, one of the primary areas of dispute for the (now politicized) "Founding Fathers" was slavery. How should the issue of slavery be addressed in a document founded on freedom? Delegates from South Carolina and Georgia, strong advocates of the slave trade, declined ratifying the Constitution until their demands for protection of the institution of slavery were met. In response, a compromise was reached. It included a twenty-year extension of the slave trade in America, a fugitive slave law, and a provision that each slave be counted as only three-fifths of a person for the basis of taxation and political representation. Governor Charles C. Pinckney, a delegate from South Carolina, was pleased with the compromise and went on to sign the Constitution solidifying the union or creation of the United States of America.

As a result the compromise, the U.S. Constitution, as written and signed by the Founding Fathers of the United States, was secured around the provision of slavery. At the time of signature there were expressed concerns by many delegates outside the Southern colonies that this compromise, which incorporated slavery into the very foundation of the Constitution, would prove to be, as stated by George Novack, "the chief crack in the cornerstone of the new Republic, a crack which in time might widen to a fissure capable of splitting the union apart" (Novack 1939:345).

The Civil War, a war between states, families, and communities in the United States, was fought over the institution of slavery and proved to be the fissure that nearly split the union apart. This fissure, the issue of slavery, has impacted representations of national heritage in the public forum.

Public perceptions of antebellum and postbellum plantations are influenced by depictions that posit the centrality of a master-slave dynamic without critique. Typical representations of this dynamic, such as the *Gone with the Wind* trope (Mitchell 1993 [1936]) and plantation depictions in popular epics such as *North and South* (Jakes 1982) and *Queen* (Haley and Stevens 1993), foreground an elite, white male plantation owner and marginalized black servants as key caricatures. In marketing this simplistic representation of racial hierarchy and place, black identity is fixed to notions of social place constructed around arbitrarily defined racial markers in which people identified as "white" are categorically assigned a higher status than people racialized or marked as "black" (or other than white), who are depicted as lacking agency.

Although contemporary scholarship widely negates race as a means of culturally demarcating people and affirms and advances definitions of race as a social versus biological construct (Graves 2001; Seshadri-Crooks 2000), the distinctions remain tenuous in daily applications. This inability to address/see/comprehend race as a social versus a biological construct continues to be held primarily because practices of racialization have become culturally ingrained over time and in many cases institutionalized within social structures and processes—and in many cases masked. Africans (enslaved and free), negroes, mulattos, and other people of color in America and throughout the diaspora, for example, have been historically and arbitrarily cast within this hierarchically constructed socially defined construction called race, which ascribes them as black, primarily through various and varying determinants such as skin pigmentation, hair texture, or descendant status (someone in their family lineage is identified as black), for example. However, it is through the efficient and silent operation of the process of signification (Hall 1996) or through an onslaught of cultural assumptions (packed with social-political ideas about Africa, enslaved Africans, and slavery) that those persons so classified as black become collectively marked with specific information about social place in society.

Paul Shackel proposed that there is a direct correlation among history, memory, and racism. He concludes his book *Memory in Black and White* by stating that underrepresented groups in the American story may accept the dominant interpretation, reject the dominant view, or "fight for representation in the public memory" (2003:14). Fighting for representation requires transformation in interpretations and public representations to address the historical centrality of race in America. Transformation will take place on a community by community level all across America. There is no single solution or approach that can be applied universally. However, in each case, questions will be raised that concern issues of determination with respect to what is communicated at selected sites and how and by whom. This transformation is taking place in venues and within groups charged with heritage preservation and management as a means of entering into a dialogue about the past.

In 2005, for example, MaVynee Betsch, a Kingsley descendant, had an informal museum on American Beach and conducted impromptu tours for anyone who showed up on the beach (Figure 1.2). In a 1998 interview, she said that sometimes people would be lost on the way to Amelia Island Plantation, a more upscale resort, and they would end up on American Beach. She would then give them the tour (Jackson 2009). American Beach was historically designated as the black beach and a site of leisure for African Americans during the period of segregation in the United States, when most public beaches restricted access based on race.

IDENTITY AND REPRESENTATION AT PUBLIC HISTORIC SITES

An array of works have been critical in shaping how black culture and identity have been represented in America over time (see Aptheker 1951; Dollard 1957; Du Bois 1961 [1903]; Frazier 1957 [1949]; Herskovits 1958 [1941], 1968 [1928]; Mintz and Price 1992 [1976]; Patterson 1982). However, in many instances, works on black culture and identity have not accounted for the historical contingency of their descriptions of African descended peoples and the impact in terms of issues of representation, as theorized by Trouillot (1995), nor have they attended to the dynamic nature of identity (see Jackson 2004 and 2011 for an expanded analysis). In the case of public history and cultural studies focused on communities written and disseminated about America before the 1960s, such as Robert and Helen Lynd's Middletown study (1929), African Americans have been underrepresented or even excluded.

Figure 1.2 American Beach, Florida (courtesy of author)

The work of anthropologist Michel-Rolph Trouillot (1995) demonstrates how attention to historicity—in this case, the historicity of
slavery—and its representation requires the development and application
of theoretical and methodological tools to allow history to be critically

examined and dynamically engaged. Trouillot proposes specific steps for interrogating processes of historical production and the role of power in determining which narratives get mentioned and which are silenced. He states: "Silences enter the process of historical production at four crucial moments: the moment of fact creation (the making of *sources*); the moment of fact assembly (the making of *archives*); the moment of fact retrieval (the making of *narratives*); and the moment of retrospective significance (the making of *history* in the final instance)" (Trouillot 1995:26; emphases in the original).

Such analytical tools provide templates for formulating critiques of processes that subjugate certain knowledges, as well as define ways for active participation in the construction of other forms, sites, and centers of knowledge that disrupt these silences. In other words, Trouillot's template opens a theoretical space for understanding, articulating, and critically assessing ways in which the global dispersion of African people during the period of the transatlantic slave trade (that is, the African diaspora) affect individuals, families, and communities in the present.

African diasporic criticism is a theoretical frame that shifts the discussion to an area of focus where meanings and objectives behind intellectual inquiry and research pursuits concerning black diaspora communities are examined. David Scott (1999), along with other proponents of African diasporic criticism (Apter 1991; Brown 1998, 2000; Gilroy 1993b; Hall 1996), has advocated analyses that begin by recognizing the fluidity of African diasporic cultural forms and the dynamism of African peoples. Scott refers to this process of discourse construction and analysis as the invoking of "tradition." According to Scott, "tradition is not a passive, absorptive relation between the past and the present. Rather tradition presupposes an active relation in which the present *calls upon* the past" (Scott 1999:115; emphasis in the original).

The importance of critically assessing connections between the past and the present with respect to interpretations that affect living people is also being pursued by archaeologists focused on addressing what is termed the "absent present" (Buchli and Lucas 2001). Like Collins (1991), Foucault (1980 [1972]), and Trouillot (1995), they compel scholars to uncover or make visible what has previously been left out or ignored. Just as it is critical to include descendant voices in constructing a database of knowledge to reinterpret plantation spaces, so, too, is the import of incorporating archaeological tools and methods that make available knowledge that cannot be spoken—graves, building remains, tools—but invite discussion about how people lived, labored, and organized themselves in places they considered home (for an expanded discussion see Buchli and Lucas 2001:15).

HERITAGE PRESERVATION AND PROMOTION—A
COLLECTIVE CHALLENGE

The inclusion of African American heritage and its movement from margin to center in U.S. history is itself a radical revisioning of national heritage.

—Carter (2008:134)

When President Bush signed the National Heritage Areas Act of 2006 authorizing the establishment of the Gullah/Geechee Cultural Heritage Corridor, it opened the door for a new interpretation of American history—interpretations specifically focused on African-American history and heritage. The law, which was championed by Rep. James E. Clyburn (D) of South Carolina, instructs the U.S. Secretary of the Interior to establish a Commission that will oversee the implementation of the Gullah/Geechee Cultural Heritage Corridor in order to help preserve, protect, and promote this endangered cultural group and their communities. The Corridor stretches from Jacksonville Florida, along Georgia's and South Carolina's coastlines, and into Wilmington, North Carolina.

Friendfield Plantation is located within the Gullah/Geechee Cultural Heritage Corridor. More recently, it has become known as the place where Michelle Obama, wife of Barack Obama, the first African-American elected President of the United States of America, can trace her family roots to enslaved African ancestors. It is public recognition of Mrs. Obama that connects this discussion about enslaved Africans to the present and crystallizes the significance of this story in the ongoing dialog about the history, heritage, memory, and place in America.

SUMMARY

Heritage is being discussed everywhere, and anthropology is eminently suited to take on the questions and challenges of the interaction between material culture and human experiences. The construction of more comprehensive representations of community history and heritage for public education, preservation, and interpretation in the United States, for example, will be the result of concentrated attention paid to the impact of the legacy of social policies and practices of exclusion (that is, the institution of slavery and legal segregation) by heritage professionals. In this book, I challenge scholars, practicing anthropologists, educators, business leaders and others to a critical examination of the impact of social policies institutionalizing racial hierarchy in America as it existed before the Civil Rights Act of 1964 on the public presentation, preservation, management, and interpretation of history and heritage on a national level. I join with and expand on the work of scholars focusing on processes of inclusion using descendant voices as sites of knowledge informing history and the production of history, such as the "Remembering Jim Crow" project (Chafe, Gavins, and Korstad 2001) and Chris Fennell and Paul Shackel's project at New Philadelphia in Pike County, Illinois—specifically, their work with the large multiracial farming community founded in 1836 by Frank McWorter (Fennell 2010; Gay 2008; Shackel 2011). McWorter was an enslaved African who purchased his freedom and that of others in his family, establishing one of the first African-American frontier settlements. Effective use of descendant knowledge has helped advance heritage preservation and interpretation efforts in this community.

Recovering knowledge from families and communities that have often been underrepresented in the public record yet remain central to understanding a larger more comprehensive American story is a collective charter. This larger story can be instructive.

Chapter 2

Issues in Cultural Heritage Tourism, Management, and Preservation

As we prepare to move into the twenty-first century, now is the time to build the great collections of oral and musical culture, art, and artifacts that future generations of scholars will use to understand our own era.

—Fath Davis Ruffins (1992:592), *Mythos, Memory, and History*

In fact, the growth of cultural tourism coincided with the emergence of a broader societywide appreciation of the need to protect and conserve our dwindling cultural and heritage assets. However, cultural tourism was seen as a double-edged sword by the cultural heritage management community. On the one hand, increased demand by tourists provided a powerful political and economic justification to expand conservation activities. On the other hand, increased visitation, overuse, inappropriate use, and the commodification of the same assets without regard for their cultural values posed a real threat to the integrity—and in extreme cases, to the very survival—of these assets.

—Mckercher and du Cros (2002:2), *Cultural Tourism*

Heritage is a key building block for tourism. And, in this discussion, it is a frame for contextualizing plantations as a key cultural resource within a larger more dynamic story of national heritage.

In this chapter, I focus on tensions and challenges associated with managing heritage as an asset for preservation and heritage as a product for consumption as in the case of tourism. Negotiating along this continuum of meeting cultural heritage resource management requirements and heritage tourism objectives requires recognition and acknowledgment of multiuse and multistakeholder objectives with respect to heritage initiatives. Emphasis is placed on the role that African diaspora communities in federally designated national heritage areas play in addressing issues confronted contemporarily as participants/stakeholders engaged in negotiating along a continuum that includes preserving cultural heritage resources and promoting these same resources for use in public consumption activities.

Within the heritage industry a distinction exists between heritage employed/viewed as an asset for conservation/preservation and heritage constructed as a product/commodity to be sold or consumed. Managing multiuse objectives among stakeholders and between local community interests and stakeholders interested in large-scale public works and development projects involves a conscious recognition of the role that power plays in mediating issues of identity and representation with respect to cultural heritage preservation and management. Different costs/benefits apply across local communities, selected populations, and variably funded stakeholders, for example. Definitions for cultural heritage tourism and cultural heritage management as interrogated by Erve Chambers (2010) and McKercher and du Cros (2002) create a common vocabulary for further discussion and analysis.

Cultural Heritage Tourism

There are many definitions of *cultural heritage tourism*. McKercher and du Cros focus on cultural tourism in terms of four elements: "(1) tourism, (2) use of cultural heritage assets, (3) consumption of experiences, and products, and (4) the tourist" (2002:6). A key point in all definitions is that cultural heritage tourism describes a type of tourism activity aimed at attracting visitors or tourists to a host location resulting in contact between visitors and hosts (Figure 2.1). However, contact between tourists and the local community represents one part of the tourism experience. The other defining aspect recognizes tourism as being a mediated experience—a highly managed experience focused on attracting to visitors typically unfamiliar with the asset being visited. Chambers underscores this point clearly, stating that:

> On almost every level imaginable, tourism is a highly *mediated* activity. It is mediated by representatives of an industry that is among the largest in the world—ranging from government officials, tourism planners, advertising and marketing agencies, associated "hospitality" industries such as the hotel and transportation companies, travel agents and guides,

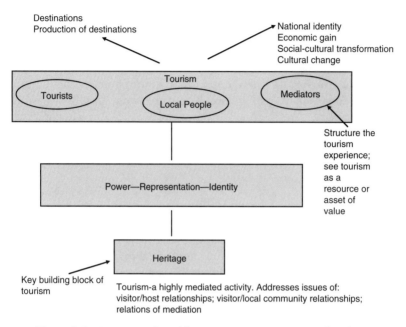

Figure 2.1 Issues in cultural heritage tourism (courtesy of author)

travel writers and publishers, preservationists, and even people who study tourism. Neither hosts nor guests in any tangible way, these individuals and agencies play important roles in determining where tourists go as well as what they see and do when they arrive at their destinations. (2010:32)

Cultural Heritage Management

Cultural heritage management includes the management of heritage as a resource consisting of tangible and intangible assets identified and conserved for their intrinsic value to a community rather than as a resource valued as a product to be sold to tourists (McKercher and du Cros 2002). Although many decisions concerning heritage resources are driven by the demands of tourism, these assets are typically governed by the regulations of cultural heritage management (CHM)—a series of codes and charters dictated by specific legislation and conventions such as the UNESCO Convention Concerning the Protection of World Cultural and Natural Heritage (1972). The discussion of the historical trajectory of archaeological heritage management presented by Henry Cleere (1989:11) states that "the basis of all archaeological heritage management must be the identification and recording of that heritage." Additionally, archaeologist Kristian Kristiansen (1989) notes that there are opposing strategies of conservation/preservation—in situ protection and excavation, for example—which must be taken into account. And Joachim Herrmann (1989) further advises that problems with archaeological research and management of sites differ from one region to the next and between countries. There are no universally applicable strategies for managing heritage resources. In the United States, cultural heritage management is addressed within the scope of CRM (cultural resource management). This process or technique of oversight generally consists of a series of protective measures aimed at sustaining and preserving the asset for the enjoyment and use of present and future generations.

Cultural Preservation

In addition to the definition of cultural heritage management presented, there are issues that are representative of experiences encountered by living communities in the context of heritage management that are best articulated in a more specific definition. I define *cultural preservation* as the act and activity of sustaining living communities or creating an environment for communities to sustain cultural practices and traditions in a manner they deem appropriate and representative of their interests. This definition includes, but is not limited to facilitating intergenerational dialog and engaging youth in culturally sustaining practices; language education/preservation; learning/applying archaeological tools/methods for marking, naming, and identifying tangible and intangible sites/resources of significance; honoring ancestors and elders; and educating visitors. The Gullah/Geechee Cultural Heritage Corridor provides a contemporary example of how living communities address heritage management and cultural preservation issues and negotiate multiple stakeholder concerns.

African Diaspora Communities in Federally Designated National Heritage Areas

National Heritage Areas are places where natural, cultural, historic, and scenic resources combine to form a cohesive, nationally important landscape arising from patterns of human activity shaped by geography. These patterns make National Heritage Areas representative of the American experience through the physical features that remain and the traditions that have evolved in them. These regions are acknowledged by Congress for their capacity to tell important stories about our nation.

—National Park Service (Gullah/Geechee Cultural Heritage website)

Federally designated national heritage areas are sanctioned by Congress to tell a national story, a story considered important in constructing the history and heritage of the nation. The Gullah/Geechee Cultural Heritage Corridor is one of over forty congressionally designated National Heritage Areas (National Park Service website—Gullah/Geechee Cultural Heritage Corridor). The Gullah/Geechee Cultural Heritage Corridor recognizes important contributions made to American culture and history by Africans and African Americans known as Gullah Geechee. The Gullah Geechee are a self-identified ethnic group and community (Gibbs 2006; Matory 2005) comprising descendants of enslaved Africans primarily from rice-growing regions of West Africa who were brought to the United States to work on large plantations focused on the production of a single cash crop such as rice, indigo, or cotton. The isolation of many of these barrier or Sea Island Plantation communities enabled the Gullah Geechee people to maintain their own unique language (Gullah) and spiritual practices, as well as other skills and traditions, including culinary, basket sewing, and fishing traditions and expertise in the cultivation of rice and other crops (Bailey 2000; Cross 2008; Daise 1986; Goodwine 1998; Hess 1992; Pollitzer 1999; Turner 2002 [1949]). A Commission was appointed to oversee the process of making the congressional mandate (the Gullah/Geechee Cultural Heritage Act)—to help preserve, protect, and promote this endangered cultural group and their communities—a reality (Figure 2.2).

The Gullah/Geechee Cultural Heritage Corridor stretches more than 12,000 square miles from northern Florida, through Georgia and South Carolina, and into Wilmington, North Carolina—including U.S. barrier islands and coastal regions along the Atlantic Ocean. In 2006 it was designated as a National Heritage Area by President Bush, making it the first and largest such federally designated land area focused on the history, heritage, and culture of people of African descent, including descendants of enslaved Africans. Many of the plantations and associated communities researched for this book, such as Friendfield, fall within this National Heritage Area, which is an excellent vantage point from which to critically analyze contemporary issues in cultural heritage preservation, resource management, and tourism—issues faced within this National Heritage Area will be a significant factor in determining how other sites of national import construct and tell a more representative, and in many instances a more complex, story of U.S. American history.

The Role of the Commission with Respect to a National Heritage Area

The role of the Commission is to articulate a vision, mission, and purpose and to create a plan for how the national heritage area is to be managed. In addition to the charter to oversee the process of making the

Gullah/Geechee
Cultural Heritage Corridor
South Carolina
Georgia
North Carolina
Florida

What is a National Heritage Area?

A National Heritage Area (NHA) is a locally-managed place designated by the United States Congress where natural, cultural, historic and recreational resources combine to form a cohesive, nationally-distinctive landscape arising from patterns of human activity shaped by geography. These areas are built on community partnerships and are planned around a region's shared heritage.

How is a National Heritage Area Different From a National Park?

The designation has both tangible and intangible benefits. Heritage conservation efforts are grounded in a community's pride in its history and traditions, and in residents' interest and involvement in retaining and interpreting the landscape for future generations. Preserving the integrity of the cultural landscape and local stories means that future generations will be able to understand their relationship to the land. Heritage areas provide educational and inspirational opportunities which encourage residents and visitors to stay in a place.

Vision/Mission/Purpose

Vision:
To recognize and sustain an environment that celebrates the legacy and continuing contributions of Gullah/Geechee people to our American heritage.

Mission:
The Gullah/Geechee Cultural Heritage Corridor Commission is committed to:
• nurture pride and facilitating an understanding and awareness of the significance of Gullah/Geechee history and culture within Gullah/Geechee communities;
• sustain and preserving land, language, and cultural assets within the coastal communities of South Carolina, Georgia, North Carolina, and Florida; and
• educate the public on the value and importance of Gullah/Geechee culture.

Purpose:
The purpose of the Gullah/Geechee Cultural Heritage Corridor is to:
• recognize the important contributions made to American culture and history by African Americans known as the Gullah/Geechee who settled in the coastal counties of South Carolina, Georgia, North Carolina, and Florida;
• assist State and local governments and public and private entities in South Carolina, Georgia, North Carolina, and Florida in interpreting the story of the Gullah/Geechee and preserving Gullah/Geechee folklore, arts, crafts, and music; and
• assist in identifying and preserving sites, historical data, artifacts, and objects associated with the Gullah/Geechee for the benefit and education of the public.

For more information about the Gullah/Geechee Cultural Heritage Corridor or the Gullah/Geechee Cultural Heritage Corridor Commission, please contact: **Michael Allen**
Charles Pinckney National Historic Site
1214 Middle Street
Sullivans Island, SC 29482
843-881-5516 x-12

Michael_allen@nps.gov

National Park Service
U.S. Department of the Interior

Figure 2.2   Gullah/Geechee Cultural Heritage Corridor (National Park Service website—Gullah/Geechee Cultural Heritage Corridor)

congressional mandate a reality, the Gullah/Geechee Cultural Heritage Corridor (GGCHC) Commission was appointed to represent and advocate on behalf of a living community. It is a community that is being marketed and interpreted as a heritage asset of significance in telling a national story. The marketing of this heritage asset is aimed at attracting visitors to, and educating local residents within, the 12,000-square-mile Corridor. The work of the Commission underscores critical intersections that mark heritage tourism as a mediated experience. This work by the Commission in exposing the fluid nature of heritage resource management/heritage tourism is important, because the idea of representing something as dynamic as culture, the Gullah Geechee culture, using processes oriented around producing fixed or static representations of assets and products is a challenging endeavor requiring active negotiation between multiple stakeholders.

The Role of the National Park Service with Respect to National Heritage Areas

According to the National Park Service (NPS), they have the responsibility to "provide technical, planning and limited financial assistance to National Heritage Areas. Rather than own or directly manage the land, the Park Service acts as a partner and advisor, leaving ultimate decision-making authority in the hands of local people and organizations" (National Park Service website—Gullah/Geechee Cultural Heritage Corridor).

The Role of Local Communities and Organizations in the Management Process

The role of affected communities is to hold the Commission and NPS accountable for creating a management plan with directives that aim to preserve the cultural heritage asset (the Corridor) and that celebrates the legacy and continued contribution of the Gullah Geechee people. Communities articulate their vision and ideas to the Commission. These ideas are fed into the inventory process, which in turn dictates the development of interpretive themes representing the Corridor.

Written records provide one means of accounting for daily life in antebellum and postbellum plantation community settings. However, sole reliance on written sources to describe plantation life yields a distorted portrait—largely based on the visions of the slave-owner elite. Charles Joyner, a noted historian specializing in southern life and culture advocates a more interdisciplinary approach: "Each type of source has its limitations, but by testing each against other types of sources and against analytical methods from other disciplines, I believe we can extend our knowledge of past folklife and make possible a quite different understanding of the slaves from their usual caricature" (1977:xivii). Thus public participation is vital to the national heritage area management process.

Oral histories, ethnographic interviews, and observation and participation by people, particularly descendants of enslaved Africans, with a vested interest in the representation and interpretation of their communities are important ways of gaining new knowledge and expanding ways of talking about Africans in plantation spaces. They provide what Geertz (1973) calls "thick description," which results in possibilities for inclusion of multiple perspectives and more nuanced details. In terms of National Heritage Area management, this process is evoked on a formal basis through listening sessions/forums termed Public Involvement Strategy sessions. National Heritage Area management teams (that is, the Commission) or their designated managing entities are required to host meetings in local communities for the purpose of soliciting input and listening to their concerns—including collecting stories and feedback regarding the management oversight process. This feedback is recorded, stored, and analyzed. A database of community feedback, as well as analysis of the collected data for the Gullah/Geechee Cultural Heritage Corridor, is managed and made publically available to the community by NPS (see National Park Service website—Planning, Environment, & Public Comment [PEPC] database).

MEETING THE FEDERAL MANDATE FOR A NATIONAL HERITAGE AREA—A LIVING COMMUNITY MODEL

The Gullah/Geechee Cultural Heritage Corridor Commission (GGCHCC) includes recognized experts in the fields of historic preservation, anthropology, history, and folklore. NPS and the State Historic Preservation Officers for the states of Florida, Georgia, North Carolina, and South Carolina nominated the Commission members, who were then appointed by the U.S. Secretary of the Interior. Part of the charter of the fifteen-member Gullah/Geechee Cultural Heritage Corridor Commission is to develop a General Management Plan (GMP) within a designated timeframe. The GMP is an agreement between stakeholders—including the National Park Service, the public, elected officials, donors, and other agencies—on what is going to be achieved over the life of the project. This is a plan that tells the world, and specifically the chief stakeholder and advisor, the National Park Service, how the Corridor, as a designated National Heritage Area, will conduct the business of heritage management as mandated by Congress in the Gullah/Geechee Cultural Heritage Act. It addresses such questions as: What is our strategy? What business, economic, cultural, and educational processes do we intend to put in place for preserving, protecting, and promoting the cultural, material, and environmental heritage of the area identified as the Gullah/Geechee Cultural Heritage Corridor?

The General Management Plan is a document that, will explain exactly how the Commission plans to organize, solicit funding, and draw on resources to fulfill the mission as defined in the charter. However, the GMP is a written document, fixed in time, whereas the role of the Commission is to remain active, continually advocating on behalf to the community. In the case of the Gullah/Geechee Cultural Heritage Corridor, for example, the advocacy role was made clear in a report prepared and submitted to the Commission by one of the subcommittee teams concerning the process for developing partnership relationships that involve as well as affect Gullah Geechee communities. In this sub-committee report, Commissioners state:

> We must be able to go into communities and "listen eloquently." In part-nering and contracting for services, we MUST reserve some of our re-sources and utilize those to educate our own communities and develop strategies of listening to and recording the elders.

> Our purpose as a Commission contains two vital words—"recognize" and "assist." Thus, as we recognize the value that each of our people and that our culture has, we are to go and assist the Gullah/Geechee people and those agencies that will effect the lives of Gullah/Geechee people.
> —Commissioners J. Herman Blake and M. Goodwine (GMP Criteria Requirements Report—"Strengthening Our Communities"—submitted November 5, 2008)

My colleagues on the Commission, many of whom are Gullah Geechee, continually demonstrate to me, beyond an academic sense, what an exercise in interpretation and management of a federally des-ignated National Heritage Area focused on a living culture is all about. Commissioner Ronald Daise from South Carolina shared the following account of his experience as a participating observer/guide on a Gullah/Geechee Heritage Tour that took place along a segment of the Corridor stretching from Charleston to Georgetown, South Carolina, on June 28, 2010. The event was marketed as a preconference tour, and it took place during the start of the International Heritage Development Conference held in Charleston, South Carolina:

> As the tour bus whirred round-trip along Highway 17 from Charleston to Georgetown, SC, a unique educational experience occurred. Forty-three 2010 International Heritage Development Conference attendees gained an authentic pre-conference "taste" of Gullah/Geechee history, heritage, and culture.

JC [a participant on the tour], of Washington, D.C., cited the June 28 event as "a very insightful and engaging session!" It was planned by Michael Allen, NPS Community Partnership Specialist, along with South Carolina members and the administrative assistant of the Gullah/Geechee Cultural Heritage Corridor Commission.

"My first priority when planning this event," said Allen, "was to present an accurate picture of the history, heritage, and legacy of a people. I knew on the bus tour would be an array of heritage area folks and community members from around the country who may never have visited or had any authentic information about Gullah culture or heritage. I wanted them to see the remnants, residues, and vestiges of the culture, as well as the threats that the culture is facing today. And, then I wanted them to celebrate the culture's victories. By that, I mean I wanted others to see some of the tangible places in the culture that weren't acknowledging or celebrating Gullah/Geechee heritage just some 15 years ago."

As the bus crossed the Cooper River Bridge, Allen informed participants that this waterway is symbolic of the Africans' arrival, their being dispersed, and their survival. The next stop was the Sweetgrass Cultural Arts Pavilion at Memorial Waterfront Park in Mt. Pleasant. Ms. Thomasena Stokes-Marshall, Executive Director, Sweetgrass Cultural Arts Festival, enlightened attendees about the history, heritage, and artistry of the popular Gullah/Geechee sweetgrass craft. Basketmakers showcased this "African art form and Lowcountry tradition."

Commissioner Green, a native, or *bin yah* (Gullah for "been here") of McClellanville, gave personal reflections about her home community while attendees toured the grounds at McClellanville's historic Bethel A.M.E. Church. The cypress shingles adorning the edifice, from which Green recalls hearing lively spirituals as she approached for services, endear it as place of spirituality. Hurricanes have not felled it. Insect infestations have not deteriorated it. Afterward, as the bus rolled toward Georgetown, attendees saw former rice plantation/landscape sites along the Santee River Delta. Rice trunks, hand-built from bald cypress wood by enslaved Africans along these abandoned rice fields, were used to flood and drain the fields of freshwater along the tidal inlets.

Commissioner Daise, a native of St. Helena Island, SC, and Vice President for Creative Education at Brookgreen Gardens, presented cultural connections of Gullah/Geechee people and their enslaved West African ancestors through song and recollections of his journeys to two West African countries. "Dats right, I am a Gullah!/a saltwater Geechee/Gullah" Daise led the participants in singing and clapping. The lyrics of his composition revealed 10 cultural touchstones about Gullah/Geechee heritage.

—Commissioner Ronald Daise (excerpt from "Gullah/Geechee
Traditions Tour Visits Georgetown County" report/article—Personal
communication with author September 29, 2010)

The tour engaged participants in the realities of a living community that
is continually writing its future.

Additionally, I am reminded of a particularly poignant moment that
took place at one the quarterly Commission meetings. I admit that it
is most likely the anthropologist in me that makes this recollection
stand out. Or, as one of my colleagues and fellow anthropologist on the
Commission puts it: "Those darn anthropologists, there you go again,
tossing around words such as agency, critique, reflexive positioning,
interpretation, and power." In other words, for a cultural anthropologist everything can potentially be viewed through an ethnographic lens.

At this particular Commission meeting, I watched a debate ensue
about the placement of specific cultural heritage resources into designated inventory categories—one of the required activities or outputs of
the General Management Plan process. The cultural resource inventory
includes the natural, historic, cultural, educational, scenic, and recreational resources of the National Heritage Area related to the stories
and themes of the region that should be protected, enhanced, managed,
or developed. Development of the cultural resource inventory is a substantive task with many implications. NPS guidelines require that the
Commission inventory cultural, material, and environmental resources
contained within Gullah/Geechee communities across all four states in
the Corridor. All items and resources recognized as significant to the
Corridor and its interpretation are to be placed on the inventory list
under categories deemed to best describe its meaning within the community where it is geographically located. In this exercise, the categories
used were developed within the context of principles/rules/regulations
as dictated by entities chartered with cultural heritage management
(CHM). These categories are parts of systems of cultural asset naming
practices that have a long history of use and relevance by groups such
as UNESCO. Items placed on the inventory list are considered to be
important assets to be preserved, protected, and promoted as essential
articulations of the Gullah/Geechee culture within the Cultural Heritage
Corridor. As you can imagine, this is a massive undertaking.

The production of a cultural resource inventory means an engagement
in an exercise that mandates distilling an entire culture—in this case, the
entire Gullah/Geechee Cultural Heritage Corridor and an entire group
of people and their cultural and heritage resources down to an itemized list organized within predefined categories. At this particular meeting, Commissioners were presented with a chart (Figure 2.3) showing

General Management Plan Committee
Inventory Sub-Committee

Inventory Categories and Definitions[1]

Tangible Cultural Heritage (TCH)	Intangible (Living) Cultural Heritage (ICH)
Tangible heritage includes all assets that have some physical embodiment of cultural values such as historic towns, buildings, archaeological sites, cultural landscapes and cultural objects, or items of movable cultural property.[2]	Intangible heritage are the practices, representations, expressions, knowledge, skills—as well as the instruments, objects, artifacts and cultural spaces associated therewith—that communities, groups and, in some cases, individuals recognize as part of their cultural heritage. This intangible cultural heritage, transmitted from generation to generation, is constantly recreated by communities and groups in response to their environment, their interaction with nature and their history, and provides them with a sense of identity and continuity, thus promoting respect for cultural diversity and human creativity.[3]
I. Monuments Architectural works, works of monumental sculpture and painting, elements or structures of an archaeological nature, inscriptions, cave dwellings and combinations of features, which are of outstanding universal value from the point of view of history, art or science	**I. Language**
	II. Oral Traditions and Expressions Oral traditions and expressions encompasses an enormous variety of forms including proverbs, riddles, tales, nursery rhymes, legends, myths, epic songs and poems, charms, prayers, chants, songs, dramatic performances and so on. They transmit knowledge, values and collective memory and play an essential role in cultural vitality; many forms have always been a popular pastime.
II. Buildings or Groups of Buildings Buildings or groups of separate or connected buildings which, because of their architecture, their homogeneity or their place in the landscape, are of outstanding universal value from the point of view of history, art, or science	Some types of expressions are common and can be used by the entire community; some are used by restricted groups, for instance among adult women only. In many societies, performing oral traditions is a highly specialized occupation, with professional performers often held in high esteem as the guardians of collective memories.
III. Sites Works of man or the combined works of nature and of man, and areas including archaeological sites which are of outstanding universal value from the historical, aesthetic, ethnological or anthropological points of view	**III. Performing Arts** The expressions central to the performing arts include especially vocal or instrumental music, dance, and theatre, but there are indeed many other traditional forms such as pantomime, sung verse, and certain forms of storytelling.
	A. Music Music is of course the most often encountered of the performing arts, found in every society and in most cases as an integral part of other performing art forms and other domains of ICH such as rituals, festive events, or oral traditions. We find it in the most diverse contexts: profane or sacred, classical or popular, closely connected to work, entertainment, even politics and economics that may call upon music to recount a people's past, sing the praises of a powerful person, or accompany or facilitate commercial transactions. The occasions on which it is performed are equally varied: marriages, funerals, rituals and initiations, festivities, all kinds of entertainment, or other social practices.
IV. Physical and Biological Formations or Groups of Such Formations Natural features which are of outstanding universal value from the aesthetic or scientific point of view	
V. Geological and Physiographical Formations Precisely delineated areas which constitute the habitat of threatened species of animals and plants of outstanding universal value from the point of view of science or conservation	**B. Dance** Dance may be described simply as ordered bodily expression, often with musical accompaniment, sung or instrumental. Apart from its physical aspect, the rhythmic movements, steps, or gestures of dance often serve to express a sentiment or mood or to illustrate a specific event or daily act, such as religious dances or those depicting hunting, warfare, or even sexual activities.
VI. Natural Sites or Precisely Delineated Natural Areas Areas of outstanding universal value from the point of view of science, conservation or natural beauty.	

Figure 2.3

C. Traditional Theater Performances

Traditional theatre performances often combine acting, singing, dance and music, dialogue, narration or recitation, but also include puppetry of all kinds as well as pantomime. These arts should perhaps not only be thought of as "performances" like those on a stage. In fact, many traditional music practices are not carried out for an external audience, such as songs accompanying agricultural work or music that is part of a ritual. In a more intimate setting, lullabies are sung to help a baby sleep.

D. Related Instruments, Objects, Artifacts and Cultural Spaces

The instruments, objects, artifacts, and cultural spaces associated with intangible expressions and practices. In the performing arts, this includes for example musical instruments, masks, costumes and other body ornaments used in dance, and the scenery and props of theatre. Performing arts are often performed in specific places; when such spaces, built or natural, are closely linked to those expressions, we may speak of cultural spaces in the Convention's terms.

IV. **Social Practices, Rituals and Festive Events**

Social practices, rituals and festive events are habitual activities that structure the lives of communities and groups and that are shared by and relevant for large parts of them. They take their meaning from the fact that they reaffirm the identity of practitioners as a group or community. Performed in public or private, these social, ritual and festive practices may be linked to the life cycle of individuals and groups, the agricultural calendar, the succession of seasons or other temporal systems. They are conditioned by views of the world and by perceived histories and memories. They vary from simple gatherings to large-scale celebratory and commemorative occasions. While each of these subdomains is vast in and of itself, there is also a great deal of overlap between them.

Rituals and festive events, which usually take place at special times and places, often call a community's attention to worldviews and features of past experience. Access may be limited in the case of certain rituals; many communities know initiation rites or burial ceremonies of this sort. Festive events often take place in public space without limitations on access—carnivals are a well-known example, and festivities marking New Year, the beginning of Spring or the end of harvest are common in all regions of the world.

Social practices shape everyday life and are known, if not shared, by all members of a community. In the framework of the Convention, attention may be paid to social practices that have a special relevance for a community and that are distinctive for them, providing them with a sense of identity and continuity. For instance, in many communities greeting ceremonies are casual, but they are quite elaborate in others, serving as a marker of identity. Similarly, practices of giving and receiving gifts may vary from casual events to important markers of authority, dependence or allegiance.

Social practices, rituals and festive events involve a dazzling variety of forms: worship rites; rites of passage; birth, wedding and funeral rituals; oaths of allegiance; traditional legal systems; traditional games and sports; kinship and ritual kinship ceremonies; settlement patterns; culinary traditions; designation of status and prestige ceremonies; seasonal ceremonies; gender-specific social practices; hunting, fishing and gathering practices; among others. They also encompass a wide variety of expressions and material elements: special gestures and words, recitations, songs or dances, special clothing, processions, animal sacrifice, special foods.

Figure 2.3 *(Continued)*

V.	**Knowledge and Practices Concerning Nature and the Universe** Knowledge and practices concerning nature and the universeinclude knowledge, know-how, skills, practices and representations developed and perpetuated by communities in interaction with their natural environment. These cognitive systems are expressed through language, oral traditions, attachment to a place, memories, spirituality, and worldview, and they are displayed in a broad complex of values and beliefs, ceremonies, healing practices, social practices or institutions, and social organization. Such expressions and practices are as diverse and variegated as the socio-cultural and ecological contexts from which they originate, and they often underlie other domains of ICH as described by the Convention. This domain encompasses numerous areas such as traditional ecological wisdom, indigenous knowledge, ethnobiology, ethnobotany, ethnozoology, traditional healing systems and pharmacopeia, rituals, foodways, beliefs, esoteric sciences, initiatory rites, divinations, cosmologies, cosmogonies, shamanism,possession rites, social organizations, festivals, languages, as well as visual arts.
VI.	**Traditional Craftsmanship** Traditional craftsmanship seems in many ways to be the most tangible of domains in which intangible heritage is expressed, but the focus of the Convention is not on craft products as such, but rather on the skills and knowledge crucial for their ongoing production. Any efforts to safeguard traditional craftsmanship must focus not on preserving craft objects—no matter how beautiful, precious, rare or important they might be—but on creating conditions that will encourage artisans to continue to produce crafts of all kinds, and to transmit their skills and knowledge to others, especially younger members of their own communities. Traditional craftsmanship is expressed in many forms: clothing and jewelry to protect or adorn the body; costumes and props required for festivals or performing arts; objects used for storage, transport, and shelter; decorative arts and ritual objects; musical instruments and household utensils; toys meant to amuse or educate, and tools vital to subsistence or survival. Many such objects are ephemeral, intended to last only as long as the community festival or family rite for which they are made. Others become keepsakes, handed down as precious heirlooms and used as models for ongoing creativity. The skills and knowledge required for artisanry to continue are sometimes as delicate as a paper votive or sand drawing, but often as robust and resilient as a sturdy basket or thick blanket.

[1] Chart based on documents submitted to me by Dr. Antionette Jackson on 10/26/08.
[2] Cultural Tourism: The Partnership between Tourism and Cultural Heritage Management by: Bob McKercher and Hilary du Cros © 2002, p.65.
[3] Convention for the Safeguarding of the Intangible Cultural Heritage 2003.

Figure 2.3 Excerpt from General Management Plan (GMP) Inventory categories report submitted November 5, 2008 (courtesy of author)

a list of categories. Our instruction on how to proceed stated that resources/assets to be inventoried were first to be identified as belonging to one of two broad categories: tangible or intangible. Next the proposed asset was to be placed under one of an array of subcategories under one of the two broad designations. As the exercise proceeded, Commissioners began offering suggestions about what asset/resource belonged where and why based on brief definitions they were given for each category and subcategory. As mentioned, the goal was to fit every resource identified as important into a particular category. Throughout the exercise there was lively discussion about what should be placed where, and many examples were offered. However, ideas about what a particular item represented to a particular Commissioner often failed to easily fit within any one category. As a result, the exchange between Commissioners became increasingly animated and passionate regarding placement of items with multiple interpretations until finally the Chair of the Commission called a halt to the process and suggested the inventory be completed in a separate series of meetings.

For an anthropologist, the inventory debate was illuminating and instructive. There I sat, in the middle of discussions and conversations about how to generate an inventory line item for identified cultural assets, per the requirements of the National Park Service's General Management Plan directive, with a highly engaged and responsive group of Commissioners (many of whom identify as Gullah/Geechee). This engagement in critiquing status quo expectations for GMP development that I was witnessing as a participant observer forced me to think about cultural heritage preservation more critically. Such an exercise highlighted the role of power in representations of national heritage in interesting and complex ways—harkening back to issues raised by Chambers (2010) and McKercher and du Cros (2002) concerning the highly mediated, gatekeeper aspects of tourism and asset preservation initiatives.

SUMMARY

The static representation of dynamic processes is an issue of particular concern for living communities engaged in heritage management and preservation. Distilling plantation sites, materially and culturally, into itemized lists and fixed themes for public branding of the visitor experience has definite impacts on a community level. There are a variety of tools and theoretical approaches that can be applied when one is addressing issues of power and representation as they pertain to stakeholders engaged in heritage resource management on a public scale. In this chapter, primacy is given to living communities as sites of knowledge for informing contemporary issues/problems in cultural/heritage management.

Knowledge articulated by descendants of enslaved Africans, which in this case also includes members of the Gullah/Geechee Cultural Heritage Corridor Commission and residents of communities located throughout the Gullah/Geechee Cultural Heritage Corridor, help develop more nuanced understandings of plantations. The import of this communication of knowledge by descendants of enslaved Africans living throughout the Gullah/Geechee Cultural Heritage Corridor is best explained by scholars who focus on geographies of blackness—spaces and places socially produced by the everyday lived experiences of people racially identified as black (Brown 2000; Carney 2001; Glissant and Dash 1989; McKittrick and Woods 2007). In talking about why they approach their work on black geographies and the production of space as they do, Katherine McKittrick and Clyde Woods (2007:7) write:

> This approach moves away from singling out the body, the culture of poverty, or the material "lack" implied by spatial metaphors, and it insists on reimagining the subject and place of black geographies by suggesting that there are always many ways of producing and perceiving space. To critically view and imagine black geographies as interdisciplinary sites—from the diaspora and prisons to grassroots activisms and housing patterns— brings into focus networks and relations of power, resistance, histories, and the everyday, rather than locations that are simply subjugated, perpetually ghettoized, or ungeographic.

Recognizing plantations in the context of heritage, both as an asset for preservation and a product for consumption in the construction and marketing of a national story, is approached in this book by giving primacy to the role of descendant knowledge. Descendants can play a critical role in reinterpreting plantations and plantation life beyond geographic, temporal, and socially bounded notions of place to include diaspora space. They help supply meaning to tangible and intangible sites of history and heritage.

The remaining chapters provide an expanded discussion of the role of descendant voices (that is, descendants of enslaved Africans) in constructing a rubric of knowledge informing representations of plantations contemporarily as sites of national history and heritage.

Chapter 3

Roots, Routes, and Representation—Friendfield Plantation and Michelle Obama's Very American Story

Slave cabins constitute minimal physical markers on the larger plantation landscape, typically preserved and showcased as memorials to, and testaments of, elite power. However, slave cabins on Friendfield, a former Sea Island rice plantation located in Georgetown, South Carolina, have gained national attention primarily because Mrs. Obama's family lineage has been traced to enslaved African ancestors at this site. National and international coverage of Michelle Obama's roots was extraordinary. The story broke in early October 2008. With her husband poised to become President of the United States of America, it was the biggest focus on America's history and heritage of slavery since the made for television movie, *Roots*. In a *Washington Post* article dated October 2, 2008, historian Peter Woods describes Mrs. Obama as the Alex Haley[1] of her generation (Murray 2008:C01). What makes Michelle Obama's roots and this moment of public reckoning with slavery from the vantage point of a descendent different from all other moments and all other conversations? I present this story in three parts.

Michelle Obama's Roots—Front Page News around the World

Headline news around the world boldly pronounced, proclaimed, and disseminated information about Mrs. Obama's roots. These articles describe in detail Mrs. Obama's maternal and paternal connections to

Figure 3.1 Slave cabins on Friendfield Plantation July 2010, unusual testaments to the American dream and obstacles overcome (courtesy of author)

slavery—*The Washington Post* (Murray 2008); *The London Telegraph* (Walvin 2008); *The Telegraph*, London (Leonard 2009); *The New York Times* (Swarns and Kantor 2009); *The Gazette*, Montreal (Alberts 2009); *The Mirror.co.uk* (Antonowicz 2009). The first stories to break focused on her paternal links to South Carolina and Friendfield Plantation. Later stories expanded to include her maternal links to slavery and mixed raced associations in Georgia. And still other stories stoked public attention by showing Michelle Obama's slavery connections and linking her to fellow American, Anderson Cooper, a popular host on a well-known and widely viewed news channel, CNN (Walvin 2008). The currency in such connections is that they generated interest and pulled the general public into the conversation about slavery and heritage. Recognizing that these headlines would shape future conversations about history, heritage, slavery, and race in America, I begin with the headlines.

All the familiar themes are right there in the headlines, often in bold type—slave, illiterate, roots, mixed-race, labored, journeyed, poverty, servitude, tangled legacy, and *Gone with the Wind*. However, could these

Figure 3.2 Michelle Obama, official White House portrait (courtesy of Joyce N. Boghosian, White House photographer, February 18, 2009)

stories about the ultimate American family be true? Reports indicate that Mrs. Obama did not even know much about her association with Friendfield until she reconnected with relatives during the campaign. For Mrs. Obama, this was an area of family history that was not really discussed when she was growing up in Chicago (Murray 2008).

When news about Michelle Obama's connection to slavery and a southern rice plantation hit the national and international airwaves I was immediately captivated. For me it was a lightning bolt moment, because this single story about the genealogical connections of a public figure, distilled down to headline news clips and sound bites, had managed to grab public interest and focus it on the legacy of slavery in America. It succeeded in creating a common point of entry for talking about plantations and slavery in everyday conversation. It was at once personal, extremely personal for some, and at the same time simply a story about someone else, albeit someone important, reckoning with her past and the rather brutal and uncomfortable realities of history.

However, these brutal realities were not so much ancient history as contemporary news on a global scale—"Michelle Obama's roots have been traced back to a six-year-old slave girl who was bequeathed to her owner's heirs along with a collection of household possessions and cattle" (Leonard 2009) and "New genealogical research has traced the roots of U.S. first lady Michelle Obama to a mixed-race family line that began about 1859 with a union between a 15-year-old slave girl and a white man in Georgia" (Alberts 2009). Catapulted into action by such widespread coverage about First Lady Michelle Obama's connection to Friendfield Plantation and slavery, I began to revisit my own interest in the topic. Her story was the catalyst I had been waiting for, because it awakened a sense of urgency in so many to learn more.

Because of Mrs. Obama's roots, there is a public scramble to openly examine the history and heritage of transatlantic slavery in America and other associations to plantations. Because of her roots, it is all right to make conversation, amends, apologies, or perhaps even memorials to this history. Mrs. Obama's kinship opens the door for critical interpretation of heritage in America, because her story helps bring into context other, not so public, links people have with the history and heritage of slavery in America.

FRIENDFIELD TODAY—AN INVESTOR'S DREAM, AN ANCESTRAL HOME, AND A NATIONAL HISTORIC PLACE

An Investor's Dream

Since Daniel K. Thorne bought into Friendfield Plantation four years ago, he has cleared its roads and drainage ditches, restored its two largest houses, and tended its forests and patches for quail.

He also pushed to have the 3,300-acre property—an area about the size of Georgetown, which lies just to the east—listed on the National Register of Historic Places. His move brought public recognition and protection to one of the state's most complete surviving rice plantations.

—Robert Behre, *The Post and Courier*, Charleston, South Carolina,
July 27, 1997

The Friendfield Plantation described in this excerpt taken from a newspaper article in *The Post and Courier* profiles a site absent of any mention of family associations that some ten plus years later, in 2008, would thrust the plantation into headline news around the world (Behre 1997). Rather, the 1997 article focuses on the business dreams of the new plantation owner and the many changes made to plantation under his tenure. The owner, Daniel K. Thorne, who had bought the 3,300 acre plantation in 1993, had succeeded over the course of four years in having the site put on the National Register of Historic Places. In the article, it is clear that his thoughts focused on how to make the plantation pay for itself as an investment. But, it would be a descendant of one of the enslaved Africans that worked for Dr. Alexius Forster and his wife Elizabeth Warham, owners of the plantation in 1850, named Jim Robinson, who would place Friendfield at the center of public attention and beyond Thorne's intense focus on business objectives.

During its economic peak in 1860, the plantation produced 658,000 pounds of rice (Behre 1997). The land later became used primarily for farming and duck and quail hunting. In late nineteenth century, pine forests on Friendfield sustained turpentine makers, and in the early twentieth century there was a fish scrap, oil, and fertilizer plant on the plantation. Rice planting is listed as having ended on Friendfield sometime between 1939 and 1942 (National Register of Historic Places Nomination Form 1996). Today some of the land is managed for timber, primarily pine (mostly longleaf), for sale to paper companies as a means of income.

Although Friendfield is once again up for sale,[2] kinship associations linking Michelle Obama to Jim Robinson now permanently link the investment dream of Daniel K. Thorne to the family roots of America's first lady. This association has awakened a desire in people to want to know more about this antebellum plantation and Mrs. Obama's roots.

An Ancestral Home

Mrs. Obama's connections to slavery and antebellum plantation sites in the U.S. South run deep and include direct links on both her maternal and paternal side (Figure 3.3). People are interested in Friendfield because of a desire to be connected to Mrs. Obama, a public figure of historical significance. Newspaper and other media outlets stoked public interest by making slavery and heritage a tantalizing topic that could be talked about with curiosity and casual familiarity.

The Shields Family Tree

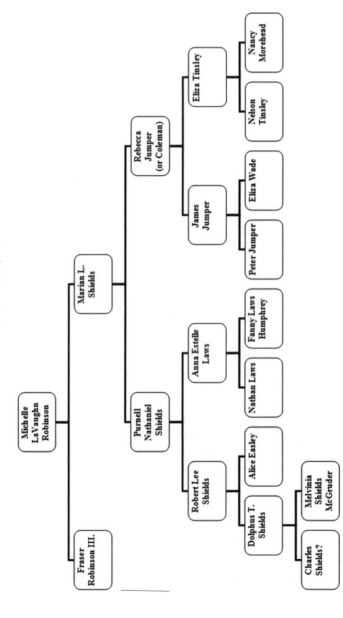

Figure 3.3a (Information compiled from census reports, property records, newspaper articles, and other historical records)

The Robinson Family Tree

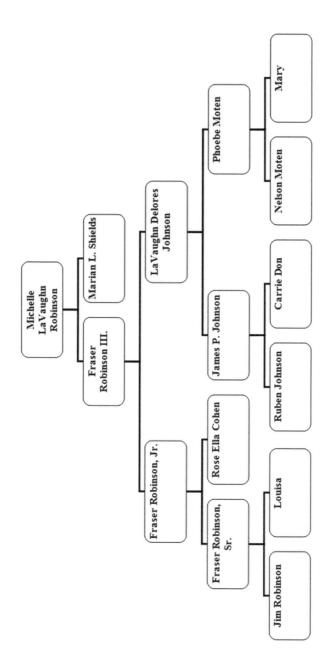

Figure 3.3b (Information compiled from census reports, property records, newspaper articles, and other historical records)

Figure 3.4 Fraser Robinson III and his wife, Marian, with their children, Craig and Michelle, now the first lady (courtesy of the Barack Obama Campaign)

On the maternal side, news stories highlight Mrs. Obama's connection to Melvinia Shields, an enslaved girl, who at age 6 was sold as part of the estate of South Carolina plantation owner David Patterson, along with a list of other possessions identified in his 1850 will. Melvinia was sold to Patterson's daughter Christianne and her husband Henry Shields, who lived in Rex, Georgia, where Melvinia was sent to live. It was here that at age 15 she gave birth to a son, Dolphus. One article marks the connection as follows; "Melvinia Shields, the enslaved and illiterate young girl, and the unknown white man who impregnated her are the great-great-great-grandparents of Michelle Obama, the first lady" (Swarns and Kantor 2009). Globally news sources repeated a similar story, with some identifying the unknown white man as Henry Shields, the plantation owner, or one of his sons. And it is Dolphus Shields' grandson, Purnell Shields (son of Robert Lee Shields and Annie Lawson), that is the father of Marion Robinson—Mrs. Obama's mother.

On the paternal side, stories highlight Mrs. Obama's connection to Friendfield Plantation through Jim Robinson. She is his great, great granddaughter. Jim Robinson was born in 1850, around the same time that Melvinia is reported as having been sold to Henry Shields. Not much is known about Jim Robinson other than that he lived on or near Friendfield most of his life and is probably buried in an unmarked grave on the plantation grounds. According to news articles, he is listed in the 1880 census as an illiterate farmhand, married to Louisa, and father of two sons, Gabriel and Fraser. His son Fraser Robinson, Mrs. Obama's great grandfather, was born in 1884 (Murray 2008). Fraser had one arm amputated as child but grew up with a determination to be educated and see his children succeed. His son Fraser Robinson, Jr., born in 1912 in South Carolina, is the father of Fraser Robinson III—Michelle Obama's father. Fraser Robinson, Jr. (who died in 1996), migrated to Chicago sometimes after 1930 but spent his retirement years with his wife, LaVaughn Robinson, in Georgetown, South Carolina. Michelle Obama and her parents visited regularly when she was growing up. Today, the Robinson family matriarch is Carrie Nelson. She is the daughter of Jim Robinson's oldest son, Gabriel.

Born in 1928, Carrie Nelson is the oldest living Robinson descendent. At age 80 she was interviewed by *Washington Post* reporter Shailagh Murray and provided critical insight into the family's past. The effect of this information was felt strongly by Mrs. Obama, whose knowledge about her family kinship, especially her connection to Jim Robinson, was first learned during the time of her husband's campaign. Murray reports the following conversation with Mrs. Obama: "If the patriarch in our lineage was one-armed Fraser, a shoemaker with one arm, an entrepreneur, someone who was able to own property, and with sheer effort and determination was able to build a life in this town—that must have been the message that my grandfather got" (Murray 2008).

Following Murray's reporting, other news sources picked up the story. For example, *The Daily Telegraph* (Australia) featured a headline that read: "Plantation to power completes family tale" and reported:

> Obama's remarkable life has seen her family go from slavery to First Lady in just four generations. Slaves helped build the White House, so Mrs. Obama's arrival there shows how much the United States has changed since then.
>
> "My past involves uncovering the shame while digging out the pride, so that other folks feel comfortable about embracing the beauty and tangled nature of the history of this country," Mrs. Obama, 45, said.
> —David Gardner, *The Daily Telegraph*, Australia, January 21, 2009

And, Anton Antonowicz (2009), reporting from Georgetown, South Carolina, in January 2009 for the *Daily Mirror* (UK), wrote about an invitation for the first lady to visit Friendfield that was extended to her by one Friendfield's current owners.

Newspaper stories and headlines retelling Mrs. Obama's "slaves in the family" story, much like Edward Ball's widely read book *Slaves in the Family* (Ball 1998), have set the stage for new interest, different interest in this southern plantation and NPS National Historic Place.

A National Historic Place

The first things I saw when I finally arrived at the entrance to Friendfield Plantation was the imposing gate, a long, isolated stretch of road leading into the plantation with no trespassing signs posted in plain view, and the NPS National Historic Register marker confirming that I had indeed arrived at the right place. I paused at the gate and tried to remember the description of the plantation that I had read on the registration form filed by the National Park Service certifying the site as a National Historic Place. The 1996 National Register of Historical Places narrative for Friendfield reads in part:

> Friendfield Plantation includes about 500 acres of former ricefields and over 2,000 acres of pine forest, mostly longleaf, managed in unevenly aged stands. Since the 1930s, the plantation has been managed as a quail preserve and winter hunting retreat. Along with the ricefields and woodlands, cultural resources on Friendfield Plantation include two significant clusters of buildings: the Friendfield House and Outbuildings and the Mount Pleasant (Silver Hill) House, Slave Street, and outbuildings. There are two historic staff residences with small-scale outbuildings, three cemeteries, several ruins with visible above ground features, and a number of known or suspected settlement sites without above-ground elements. The variety of historic uses on Friendfield Plantation is evidenced by tar kiln mounds, a fish oil and scrap factory tanks, and stones remaining at the site of a former rice mill.
>
> —National Register of Historic Places Nomination form, Friendfield Plantation, March 1996

Figure 3.5 Friendfield House entry gate, July 2010 (courtesy of author)

I visited Friendfield Plantation for the first time in May 2009 and actually toured it in July 2009. I took the occasion of my Gullah/Geechee Cultural Heritage Corridor Commission meeting, held in Georgetown, South Carolina, May 14–15, 2009, to get close and learn more. However, at this time I was inquiring about a site called Friendfield Village, which today is part of Hobcaw Barony, or Bellefield Plantation, on Waccamaw Neck between Winyah Bay and the Atlantic Ocean, in Georgetown County, South Carolina. Although this inquiry proved to be based on a case of mistaken plantation identity, it did help me learn more and get one step closer to Friendfield Plantation.

It is customary as part of the Commission meetings, that we are given a tour of the area where the meetings are being held. These tours were typically arranged by commissioners from the state hosting the meetings. The Georgetown meeting was no exception, and so I found myself on a tour of Georgetown. During this tour, our guide, Mrs. "Bunny" Rodrigues, who is extremely knowledgeable about the area through her own family's deep connections to the area, had the driver pass by the entry to Friendfield Plantation. At the entry, which is rather nondescript from the main road, Ms. Rodrigues, said, "that's Friendfield." The bus kept moving, and I looked around to get my bearings; then like many others on board, I started quickly taking pictures of the sign. Friendfield was not one of our scheduled tour stops, but as we drove by Ms. Rodrigues told us some stories about her visits to the site and her personal acquaintance with the current owners. She also mentioned that, as commissioners, we could probably get access to the site and get a tour. As the bus moved farther away from the sign and down the highway toward our next scheduled stop, she mentioned that on the way back we would again pass the Friendfield entrance, and those of us who had not gotten a good look the first time would have another chance. On the return trip, we did indeed pass the Friendfield entry sign again, and I took more pictures. I was happy to have gotten one step closer. I now knew exactly where the plantation was located.

Once back at the hotel, I was restless to go back to Friendfield and get a bit closer, so I decided to drive back by the entry. I retraced the bus route and found myself only 15 minutes from the hotel but a world away in thoughts and anticipation. I pulled up to where the bus had passed and this time proceeded down the road toward the plantation grounds. I crossed a railroad track and saw a few houses on one side of the road as I approached what looked to be the main entry point to the plantation. There was a large, very visibly posted no trespassing sign and a gate, which was open. There was also a large plaque mounted on a brick pillar that declared Friendfield to be on the United States Department of the Interior National Park Service National Register of Historic Places.

Ahead of me, and as far as my eyes could see beyond the gate, was a long road and lots of trees and brush. The quiet was calming and at the same time daunting, since it underscored my isolation. I had not mentioned to anyone that I was coming back here, and now here I stood trying to determine whether to proceed down the road, pass the open gate, and go into the area that the no trespassing sign warned me about. My heart was racing, and I decided to go only a small way pass the gate and down the deserted lane. I drove slowly and kept telling myself to turn back. I strained to see what would come next, and still I could see only trees and brush. As the gate got farther away and could barely be seen from my rear view mirror, I decided that I would just keep going until I caught a glimpse of something besides trees and brush. I prepared a statement in my mind in case I got stopped. I pulled out my Commissioner badge to substantiate my claim of legitimacy for having ventured this far. Finally I reached a fork in the road, and there was a sign showing several options, including one that said Friendfield. I went in the direction of Friendfield. Suddenly, I passed a beautiful tennis court and in the distance saw the roof of a house. I was struck by the contrast of finding a tennis court so deep in the woods, so isolated. I remembered seeing the plantation on the news, CNN I think, and they showed some slave cabins, expansive grounds, and the river. But, I had not seen a tennis court. As I passed by the courts, I suddenly saw in my rear view mirror that a pick-up truck was headed my way. I became extremely nervous and anxious and reached down to touch my badge. I pulled over to the side of the road near a small white house with a driveway. I waited for the truck to reach me. When the truck was close enough, I rolled down the window to speak to the driver. He was a white male, with a medium build, and he was wearing jeans and one of those work shirts that maintenance folks wear. He asked me what I was doing here and several times asked if I knew that this was private property. He seemed annoyed but not too menacing. I offered up my excuse. I told him that I was a Commissioner and thought that since I was here for our meetings that I thought it would be ok to take a drive around the grounds. I told him I knew that I needed to make an official appointment and indicated to him that I would do so and that I was sorry to have just wandered onto the grounds without permission. I was actually very sorry and a bit nervous to be on my way because I remembered once again that I had not told anyone of my plans to visit Friendfield. But for some reason, he suddenly said that he would drive me around if I really wanted to see a few of the buildings and perhaps the slave cemetery. I then recognized him as the groundskeeper that I had seen on television when the reporters did a story on Friendfield. My heart was beating rapidly as he waited for me to answer. I quickly gathered my camera and tape recorder and got in his truck. When we started down the road toward the plantation house and he saw my camera, he said I could not take pictures or tape anything. I told him that it was for research and that if I could not take pictures then I needed to come back when this was possible. He kept offering to show me around, and I actually became concerned about my circumstances. I was alone, deep in the woods, on a private plantation site, with a guy that I really did not know. I decided that I had actually already achieved my goal, I was at Friendfield, and I needed to get back to the hotel. He agreed to take me back and made a quick loop around a small portion of the grounds as he headed back to my car. He pointed out a few slave cabins and the area where one of the cemeteries on the grounds was located. My excitement at passing by these things momentarily made me forget my concern, and I just looked out the window at the white, dilapidated buildings—the remaining slave cabins on the site—and wondered about the people buried in the cemetery. Were the First Lady's relatives buried there? In the newspaper article it mentioned that she had often passed the front entrance near Highway 521 (Highmarket Street), where our tour bus had also passed, but had not really connected with the plantation in any way. When we reached my car, Ed, the caretaker, gave me his number and indicated I should call about two weeks before I wanted to come back for an invited visit and tour so that he could make the proper arrangements. I thanked him and headed out.

So, on July 20, 2009, I was given an "official" tour of Friendfield by the plantation caretaker, Mr. Ed Carter (see Figure 3.6, map of Friendfield). This time I invited two of my fellow Gullah/Geechee Commissioners to accompany me, and Ed was welcoming. He told me I could take pictures and use my tape recorder. Our tour started at the cemetery, and we were allowed to spend as much time as we wanted at this stop. It was the experience I hoped for and the connection I had wanted to make. As part of my research, I have visited many coastal rice plantations; however, this one was profoundly different; it linked me to the White House all the way from Slave Street on Friendfield Plantation. It linked me to the American dream through the legacy of slavery in America.

Organized tours from Charleston to Washington, D.C. showcase the grandeur of homes, estates, landscapes, gardens, and other holdings of former plantation owners such as Presidents George Washington and Thomas Jefferson and Governors Charles Pinckney and William Aiken. I have taken numerous organized tours of antebellum plantations turned tourist sites and marveled at the splendor and beauty of these picturesque places—these monuments to the institution of slavery. I have also recoiled in shame and anger at the sight of slave quarters, cottages, and cabins and at the deafening silence surrounding the history and heritage of enslaved Africans and their descendants who made these sites possible. Today Slave Street on Friendfield Plantation in Georgetown, South Carolina, has achieved

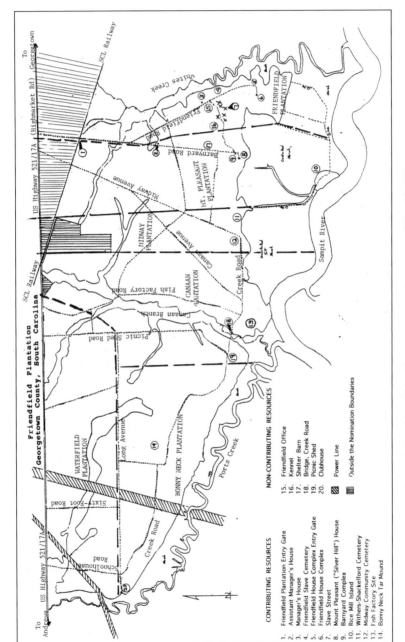

Figure 3.6 Friendfield Plantation map (courtesy of HABS/HER)

monument stature through its association with First Lady Michelle Obama. In an unprecedented moment in history, the public is looking into the life of an unknown enslaved African named Jim Robinson and connecting his history and heritage to the highest office in the land, that of the President of the United States of America, Barack Obama, and his wife, Michelle Robinson Obama. My interest in Friendfield Plantation is and was simply centered on First Lady Michelle Obama. Subsequently, I set out to visit Friendfield to connect to a historical moment—to gaze upon a monument.

ORGANIZED TOURING AND PUBLIC LOOKING

At Friendfield Plantation in Georgetown, participants visited the ancestral home of First Lady Michelle Obama (her great-great-grandfather Jim Robinson lived at Friendfield). Vermelle "Bunny" Rodrigues, a Georgetown native, historian, quilter, and co-owner of De Gullah O'oman Museum in Pawleys Island, showcased her story quilt, "The Michelle Obama Quilt, From the Slave Cabin to the White House."
—Ronald Daise, GGCHCC Commissioner, 2010:4

It's not exactly *Gone with the Wind*, but what makes this overgrown 3,300 acres of marsh and pine trees stand out is this: The family of first lady Michelle Obama believes her great-great-grandfather was held as a slave here and labored in the mosquito-infested rice fields.
—Joe Johns and Justine Redman, CNN's AC 360-CNN.com, July 16, 2009

What does an organized tour to Friendfield Plantation mean? What do visitors hope to learn about history, about heritage, about an antebellum plantation site and those who lived and worked there? On June 28, 2010, representatives from the Gullah/Geechee Cultural Heritage Corridor Commission in South Carolina led a Pre-Conference tour for the International Heritage Development Conference held in Charleston, South Carolina. One of the scheduled stops on the tour was advertised as Friendfield Plantation, Georgetown (Co.), SC "the Ancestral Home of First Lady Michelle Obama."

The International Heritage Development Conference (IHDC) is sponsored by the Alliance of National Heritage Areas (ANHA) headquartered in Washington, D.C. ANHA promotes and advocates cultural heritage tourism, highlighting distinguished examples of sustainable heritage development. The International Heritage Development Conference is an organized event that provides opportunities for communication and dialogue among directors, staff, and partners from emerging and dedicated local, state, national, and international heritage areas and others with similar landscape-scale conservation and community development interests and objectives. Participants come from around the country as well as internationally.

The roster for the 2010 Pre-Conference Tour included forty registered participants, who each paid $75.00 to participate. The business and professional affiliations of tour participants ranged from local area businesses and organizations in Charleston and surrounding communities to associations with the National Park Service, to the History Channel Magazine, to the *Philadelphia Sun News*, for example (Figure 3.7).

The Pre-Conference Tour, named HIGHWAY 17 "A Window into our History," ran from 7:15 A.M. to 4:30 P.M. and included a full itinerary of sites that were identified as: Site 1, the Cooper River Bridge; Site 2, The Sweetgrass Cultural Pavilion; Site 3, Historic Bethel AME Church and other sites in McClellanville, South Carolina; Site 4, the Santee River Delta, Charleston and Georgetown counties; Site 5, Brookgreen Gardens, Murrells Inlet, South Carolina; and the final stop, Site 6, Friendfield. Tour participants received a glossy program booklet authored/prepared by representatives of the Gullah/Geechee Cultural Heritage Corridor Commission from South Carolina that included a welcome message from Commission Chair Emory Campbell, an itinerary and description of sites to be visited, and a brief history of the Gullah/Geechee Cultural Heritage Corridor and the role of the Commission. An excerpt from the booklet profiling the Friendfield Plantation stop reads: "This landscape would not be what you see today had it not been for the perseverance and tenacity of people of African descent. Our final destination on this tour is Friendfield Plantation. We will pass dozens of plantations on this journey. Many of these plantations are now disguised as sprawling residential subdivisions, golf courses, and a range of other chosen developments" (Gullah/Geechee Cultural Heritage Corridor Pre-Conference Tour 2010).

According to information reported by participants, Friendfield Plantation was one of the highlights of the tour (Daise 2010). Lunch was

National Park Service	Silos & Smokestacks National
Central Heritage Society	Sweetgrass Cultural Arts Festival
Berkeley Chamber of Commerce	Silos & Smokestacks National
History Channel Magazine	Cane River National Heritage Area
Augusta Canal National Heritage	Delaware & Lehigh National

Figure 3.7 2010 International Heritage Development Conference and Pre-Conference Tour participants' roster (courtesy of author)

served at the Friendfield site and the welcome message in the tour booklet written by Commission Chair Emory Campbell described it as "a feast of our best Gullah dishes served at historic Friendfield Plantation—the ancestral home of First Lady Michelle Obama" (Gullah/Geechee Cultural Heritage Corridor Pre-Conference Tour 2010). The Friendfield visit also included a program of singing and praise under one of the trees on the site, as well as sharing the history of the plantation presented by Vermelle "Bunny" Rodrigues, a Georgetown native, historian, quilter, and co-owner of De Gullah O'oman Museum in Pawleys Island, and members of the Friendfield Plantation staff. Caretaker Ed Carter led interested participants on a tour of the cemetery and plantation grounds, including Slave Street, which consisted of remains of cabins where enslaved African workers and their descendants lived well into the 1970s.

The Friendfield Plantation stop and the entire Pre-Conference HIGHWAY 17 "A Window into our History" tour was a pilot heritage tourism event for the GGCHCC. It is anticipated that future antebellum plantation tours and program offerings on the history and heritage of the Gullah/Geechee culture and communities marketed and sold to the general public will reference this experience in program planning efforts.

Following the tour, a survey was taken by the South Carolina National Heritage Corridor to record participant experiences. Results indicate that, when asked about their favorite experience on the tour, many of the participants referred to the Friendfield Plantation stop as significant (Figure 3.8). Pre-Conference Tour documentation, interviews, and surveys all underscore the significance of Michelle Obama's ancestral connections to Friendfield as selling point and major point of influence in conveying information about antebellum plantations in South Carolina.

SUMMARY

Incorporating a wider range of perspectives based on narratives of descendants of enslaved Africans can help to revise or rethink static, discretely bounded portrayals of slave life and open up the space to view African communities in plantation spaces more holistically and dynamically. Friendfield Plantation is important, because the heritage of the First Lady of the United States of America, Michelle Obama, a descendant of enslaved Africans, is important. This chapter chronicles the dialogue that brought people to Friendfield and made Friendfield relevant in the public sphere in the present. The story of Friendfield Plantation is an American story of national significance. Friendfield is important beyond the specter of headline news descriptions that emphasized familiar and readily accessible plantation story tropes. It is important also because it engenders a reimagination of plantations, plantation spaces, enslaved

What was your favorite experience on this tour?

- First Lady's ancestors home visit and lunch and Sweetgrass pavilion
- The narrative history/ commentary on the G-G history, experience, culture, traditions, etc.—I learned a lot!
- Sweetgrass baskets
- The tour of Friendfield

- The Plantation, presentation/lunch

- Walking to the cemetery at Friendfield Plantation and seeing so many correlations between burial practices of people of African descent in the Carolina coastal area and those in this area of Louisiana (adjacent to water, artifacts left there, relatively active traditional cultural practices). And the interactions with people at each stop. Hearing them tell about their culture is always the best.

- Lunch and program under the tree. Thank you for making this awesome connection so we could spend time at that site.

- The detailed information of Gullah's history, i.e., folklore, traditions, language

- Lunch at the plantation

- Friendfield Plantation

Figure 3.8 Participant Survey response, 2010 International Heritage Development Conference, IHDC HIGHWAY 17 "A Window into Our History" tour (courtesy of South Carolina National Heritage Corridor)

Africans, and American history to tell a bigger, more critically engaging story. From a methodological perspective, leaving the archives to spend time in communities and with people directly affected by the stories we tell is an essential part of anthropological research and this project.

Chapter 4

JEHOSSEE ISLAND RICE PLANTATION

A World Class Ecosystem—Made in America by Africans in America

The legacy of commercial rice production on Jehossee Island and other such rice plantations in the U.S. South makes the Friendfield Plantation important beyond the specter of headline news descriptions about Michelle Obama and familiar tropes about plantations and enslaved Africans. This analysis of the legacy of commercial rice production on Jehossee Island, part of the ACE Basin National Wildlife Refuge, underscores the complex system of interdependence between Africans and Europeans, particularly evident during the period of transatlantic slavery in U.S. American history. In this chapter, I give primacy to telling the story of the role that enslaved African people played in construction and preservation of an ecosystem considered to be of world class significance today. It is an active act of heritage management and interpretation aimed at critically informing benign representations of antebellum plantation sites for tourist consumption and sensational accounts of slavery and enslaved Africans and their descendants for headline news.

* * *

The story of Jehossee Island, like the story that could be told of Friendfield Plantation, is in the rivers that irrigated rice fields planted, harvested, and managed by enslaved Africans and their descendants.

The story of Jehossee Island is in the bold beauty of the Edisto and Dawho rivers, and in small stacks of bricks intermittently piled along "slave row," marking the spot where chimneys for cabins that housed enslaved Africans and their families once stood. It is in the towering beacon of the remains of a rice mill chimney stack that stands near the trickling of a small river stream. The story is in stems and stalks of tall grasses surrounding the plantation overseer's house turned hunting lodge during the postbellum period of the 1920s, and in the marked and unmarked graves scattered throughout the quiet of the wooded grounds on Jehossee Island.

Jehossee is what you see, what you feel, and what you come to know if you listen carefully for answers to questions that the tourist brochures leave restlessly sitting in the back of your mind, such as—what were all those Africans doing on Jehossee Island rice plantation? It is in the sentiment shared by a Park Ranger who said that if he could be transported to any period in time and ask a question that he would want to go back to the period when Jehossee was a thriving rice plantation in the mid-1800s. On arrival he would ask the Africans living and working on the plantation how they protected themselves from mosquitoes. This problem remains a formidable and menacing one for anyone venturing on the island today.

Jehossee is a story of speaking for the enslaved through interpreting the history of a rice ecosystem at a National Wildlife Refuge located within the geographic boundaries of two federally designated National Heritage Areas in America—the Gullah/Geechee Cultural Heritage Corridor and the South Carolina National Heritage Corridor. The act of uncovering or questioning silences about Africans, Europeans, and rice production on one antebellum plantation is an act of recovering knowledge that has been subjugated. Subjugated knowledges are ways of knowing contained within the historical record, which critical analysis can make visible, and ways of knowing embodied within individuals and communities that have typically been ignored or disproportionately represented as peripheral (Collins 1991; Foucault 1980 [1972]). Uncovering processes in historical production that act to silence certain narratives and make others visible is an active act of intervention and interpretation (Trouillot 1995). And regardless of the reason for the silence, the impact of the act of disrupting processes that create silence is not benign.

Jehossee Island rice plantation sits at a critical intersection in which issues in heritage management, heritage tourism, and theoretical implications of power and the production of history (Trouillot 1995) are illuminated. Additionally, Jehossee underscores the significance and the requirement of viewing antebellum plantation spaces in global context or, in this case, from an African's diasporic perspective.

Sea Island rice plantations off the coast of Florida, Georgia, North Carolina, and South Carolina were a compilation of communities composed primarily of Africans and their descendants. Public tours of plantations, and associated literature and brochures distributed to visitors, typically provide one perspective—focusing on the culture, traditions, and life experiences of plantation owners and their families, while offering only generic references to slavery. For example, in public brochures about the ACE Basin National Wildlife Refuge currently being distributed by the U.S. Fish and Wildlife Service (USFWS), references are made to a tradition of land stewardship in which owners of large plantations managed their wetlands primarily to grow rice, which was followed by period of wealthy sportsmen who maintained hunting retreats and continued to keep the land and rice ecosystem in pristine condition, finally leading to today, when the refuge and its ecosystem continue to be protected and maintained. An excerpt from the U.S. Fish and Wildlife Service ACE Basin brochure presented to visitors reads: "Home to large plantations owned by a small number of individuals who managed their wetlands primarily to grow rice" (U.S. Fish and Wildlife Service—ACE Basin Refuge visitor brochure, August 2005). In such descriptions and interpretations, the complex and comprehensive role played by majority African communities in plantation management and daily operations goes unrepresented.

Yet, Africans dominated the geographic landscape in which the production of rice in U.S. Sea Island communities took place. Jehossee was no exception. Jehossee's legacy as a site of commercial rice production, now part of the ACE Basin National Wildlife Refuge, is emblematic of the labor, ingenuity, and expertise of enslaved African people and the role they played in constructing and preserving what today is considered to be an ecosystem of world class significance. It is also emblematic of benign depictions of enslaved African labor on antebellum plantations. This interpretation is aimed at critically informing benign depictions of African labor on antebellum plantation sites, which are being marketed as postbellum sites of history for tourist consumption and in the case of Friendfield, discussed in the previous chapter, for headlines and selling news.

Jehossee Island is located off the Edisto and Dawho rivers about 25 miles southeast of Charleston, South Carolina. It was the site of a thriving rice plantation in the 1800s. Jehossee was a community planned and managed around the cultivation and exportation of rice, and more than 95 percent of the people who lived and worked on the island were Africans or descendants of Africans. One of the largest plantations in South Carolina, Jehossee is most frequently referenced between the periods 1830 and 1887, when it was owned by the Governor, William Aiken.

Today Jehossee, as part of the ACE Basin National Wildlife Refuge (Figure 4.1), is owned by the United States Government and administered by the U.S. Fish and Wildlife Service. Named for the Ashepoo, Combahee, and Edisto rivers, ACE Basin is the largest estuarine resource in South Carolina and one of the largest undeveloped estuaries on the Atlantic coast of the United States. The ACE Basin Project was launched in 1998 with the stated mission of maintaining the natural character of the basin by promoting sustainable resource management. It is nationally recognized for its wide variety of recreational uses, as well as for its diversity of plants and wildlife, including being a habitat for many endangered and threatened species.

ACE Basin NWR—Edisto Unit

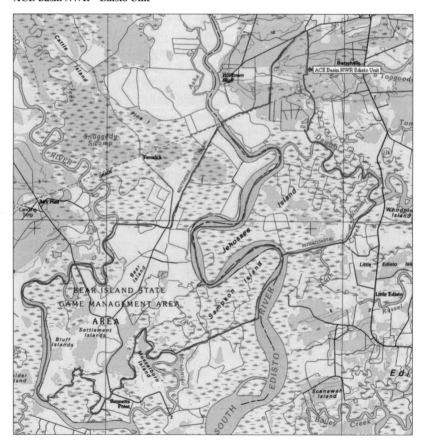

Figure 4.1 ACE Basin, including Jehossee Island (courtesy of ACE Basin NWR, Edisto Unit)

The U.S. Fish and Wildlife Service, which manages the over 11,000-acre ACE Basin National Wildlife Refuge, acquired Jehossee Island, nearly 4,000 acres, in 1993 from David H. Maybank, a descendant of William Aiken. The headquarters of the ACE Basin National Wildlife Refuge is located in the Grove Plantation House (Figure 4.2), which was built in 1828. The Grove Plantation House is recognized as one of only three mansions in the ACE Basin that survived the Civil War intact, and it has been placed on the National Register of Historic Places to ensure its continued preservation. According to the U.S. Fish and Wildlife Service (2007), the refuge has over 25,000 visitors annually and offers public-use activities such as bird watching, photography, hiking, boating, canoeing, fishing, hunting, and historical interpretation (Figure 4.3).

Jehossee is a site of primary significance within the ACE Basin National Wildlife Refuge.[1] The wetlands are considered of national and international importance primarily because the altered landscape of its rice ecosystem and undeveloped estuaries remains home to a variety of flora and fauna. Impoundments or former rice fields, now referred to as *managed wetland units*, are maintained because of their attraction as habitats for various migratory and resident birds. According to the South Carolina Department of Natural Resources (2010), ACE Basin Project History, the ACE Basin has been designated as a world class ecosystem under The Nature Conservancy's Last Great Places program.

The celebrated natural heritage of Jehossee Island is intertwined with the cultural heritage of enslaved African people and their descendants. Starting in the mid-1700s, enslaved Africans cleared and diked thousands of acres of tidal swamps bordering many of the rivers in South Carolina for the production of rice, including those in areas now managed by the ACE Basin National Wildlife Refuge, such as around Jehossee Island. A total reliance on African labor and expertise and adherence to a strict maintenance regime was the norm for planters seeking to profit from their commercial rice investment.

However, the centrality of enslaved African people in terms of their cultural knowledge, traditions, and expertise with respect to rice cultivation to date has been significantly understated. From a public awareness standpoint, the documentation distributed to the general public about the ACE Basin National Wildlife Refuge reveals nothing of their contributions. Visitors to ACE Basin National Wildlife Refuge are provided with limited information and no written documentation (pamphlets, brochures, maps, and posters) about the historical relationship and association between enslaved African people and changes made to the natural environment. In particular, the role Africans played in the building, maintenance, and preservation of rice impoundments on Jehossee Island is subjugated knowledge. It is knowledge (skills, technology, and

Figure 4.2   Grove Plantation House in 1997 (*top*) and 2007 (*bottom*)
(courtesy of author)

U.S. Fish & Wildlife Service

Ernest F. Hollings ACE Basin
National Wildlife Refuge

Mark Purcell, Refuge Manager
Ernest F. Hollings ACE Basin NWR
P.O. Box 848
Hollywood, SC 29449
Phone: 843/889 3084
Fax: 843/889 3282
Web: acebasin.fws.gov
E-mail: acebasin@fws.gov

Refuge Facts
- Established: 1990.

- Acres: 11,815.

- Made up of two separate units, the Edisto River Unit (7,200 acres) and the Combahee River Unit (4,564 acres).

- Located in Beaufort, Charleston, Colleton, and Hampton counties, SC.

- Refuge is part of the ACE Basin Project, a joint venture in which the U.S. Fish and Wildlife Service, South Carolina Department of Natural Resources, The Nature Conservancy, and Ducks Unlimited are working with private landowners to protect and enhance the natural resources of a 350,000-acre area.

- Location: refuge office is located 25 miles south of Charleston off of Highway 17. From Highway 17 take SC 174 through the town of Adams Run. At intersection with flashing light, turn right onto Willtown Road. Entrance road to refuge is approximately 2 miles on left and next to Refuge sign. Office is located in the Grove Plantation House approximately 2.2 miles down the gravel road.

Natural History
- The refuge area consists of 3,950 acres of tidal marsh, 3,000 of managed wetland impoundments, 1,200 acres of bottomland hardwoods, 2,800 acres of upland forest, and 700 acres of grass and shrublands.

- Bald eagles nest on both refuge units. Endangered wood storks utilize the area during the summer months. Concentrations of up to 30,000 ducks use the impoundments in winter months. Large numbers of wading birds, shorebirds and raptors are present in seasons.

- Songbird (neo-tropical migrants) use in all areas of uplands and bottomland forests.

Financial Impact of Refuge
- Six-person staff.

- 25,000 visitors annually (and growing).

Refuge Objectives
- Assist in the preservation of the ACE Basin area.

- Manage for migratory birds.

- Preserve, protect and manage habitats for endangered and threatened species such as wood stork, American alligator and bald eagle.

- Manage refuge for native species.

- Provide recreational and environmental education for the public.

- Provide protection and preservation of historical buildings and archaeological sites.

Management Tools
- Partnerships.

- Water management.

- Prescribed fire.

- Law enforcement.

- Building restoration/preservation.

- Timber cutting operations.

- Mechanical control of vegetation.

Public Use Opportunities
- Trails.

- Fishing.

- Hunting.

- Wildlife observation.

- Photography.

- Historical interpretation.

Figure 4.3 Ernest F. Hollings ACE Basin NWR Fact Sheet (courtesy of ACE Basin National Wildlife Refuge—www.fws.gov/acebasin/, accessed December 4, 2010)

laboring practices) embodied within the enslaved African community on Jehossee that has been disproportionately represented as peripheral and effectively silenced. These impoundments form the basis of the ecosystem that sustains the environment that attracts visitors and fuels the wide variety of advertised public-use activities (South Carolina Department of Natural Resources 2010). Africans' invisibility at Jehossee raises questions about meaning; that is, what does it mean when we emphasize one aspect of the transatlantic story of slavery, commerce, and conservation in informational material distributed to visitors at former antebellum plantation sites? What are the opportunity costs (what is gained and what is lost by stakeholders and the descendent community) of telling the story one way as opposed to another? What tools and theories can we draw on to critique the production of heritage on a national level for public consumption and distribution?

Jehossee is representative of a national story that is central to American history and heritage. Jehossee is also the story of the African diaspora. Incorporating and illuminating Jehossee's story of the interdependence of African and European people around the production and global distribution of rice at this historical/political moment coincides with the rise in awareness by public entities, such as the National Park Service. NPS is charted with telling more nuanced national stories to the general public that are representative of all communities and people, particularly those responsible for creating and sustaining locations designated as National Heritage Areas.

WHY JEHOSSEE, WHY RICE, WHY AFRICANS?

Rice as a Cultural Tradition

Africa's rich heritage of rice cultivation has benefited the world, and yet today little is known about this tradition, and few people associate rice with Africa. Rice cultivation dates back to the earliest ages of human existence, with evidence of its cultivation in West Africa documented around 1500 B.C.E. There are over twenty-five species of rice, of which two are recognized as having been domesticated: *Oryza sativa* (*O. sativa*) and *Oryza glaberrima* (*O. glaberrima*). The species *O. glaberrima* is cultivated almost exclusively in West Africa, while *O. sativa* is widely grown in tropical and subtropical regions around the world (Grist 1986 [1953]). African knowledge of rice production, however, was not unknown to European traders (Carney 1993, 2001; Littlefield 1991 [1981]; Wood 1976). Slave traders and others provisioned their ships with purchases of surplus rice obtained along the coast of West Africa from present day Gambia to Angola, sometimes referred to as the "rice coast."

From a cultural perspective, rice is very important in the lives of many Africans. The Mende people, who occupy the central and eastern part of Sierra Leone, as well as the Kissi people of the forest region of

French Guinea, for example, are essentially known as rice people. In these cultures, rice not only is a staple food and a primary crop but also has very important social value (Fields 2001, 2008; Little 1951). Coastal rice production and associated agricultural strategies and social practices developed in the western region of Africa underscore a tradition of rice cultivation in West Africa.

The introduction of West African rice traditions into antebellum plantation interpretation processes, privileges African knowledge systems, expertise, and perspectives on rice agriculture in constructing a frame of reference for analyzing environmental, agricultural, and social-cultural conditions encountered by majority African communities in coastal rice-growing regions and environments in the southeast area of the United States. In other words, from what knowledge systems did Africans possibly approach coastal rice production in the United States? What evaluative frames did they use to critique their experiences? And how should those chartered with interpretation approach their task and make Africans visible?

Development of the rice industry along the southeast coast of the United States was an act of social and environmental construction conceived on the part of European investors and the early founding families in search of a cash crop and means of generating wealth. This industry was operated, maintained, and managed by enslaved African people and their descendants. Land, people, and cultures were transformed for the sole purpose of producing a single cash crop.

A massive amount of labor and tremendous effort went into the initial clearing of swampland to transform them into a level of commercial productivity. Many of these original swamps were cypress forests that had to be cleared, after which miles of ditches, dikes, and canals were constructed to provision the huge irrigation system on which tidal swamp rice production depended. It was literally a steady influx of African labor that made the creation of these thriving rice ecosystems at Jehossee and other plantations possible. Edward Ball described the experience of the Ball family and other rice planters in this way:

> Throughout the 1780s and 1790s, the Balls and other planters directed their slaves to move the rice fields from the swamps down to the banks of streams, creating fields that made use of the tides. The process had begun in some places before the war, but it now proceeded apace. To reclaim the marsh as arable land required earthworks. First the workers constructed levees, or rice banks, around rectangular plots laid out in the mudflat. A rice bank stood about six feet high and had one or more openings so that tidewater could be admitted to the field. The flow was controlled by a large wooden sluice, or trunk, which resembled a guillotine with the

dimensions of a barn door. When opened at high tide, the trunk allowed the tide to flood the field. With the trunk closed, the water stayed on the crop. Opened again at ebb, the trunk drained the plot and the field dried hard. It may have been that this method, tidal rice farming, was brought to America by West Africans, who showed the technique to the Carolina landlords. A drawing made by an English traveler in Sierra Leone in the year 1794 shows rectangular rice fields surrounded by banks, with a portal for water to pour in and out.

—Ball (1998:249)

Once created, these artificial systems required constant maintenance to remain productive. A central feature used in controlling water flow in tidewater agriculture in the U.S. Sea Island plantations was the device, mentioned in the preceding passage, called the "trunk" (Figure 4.4). Geographer Judith Carney, who has done extensive work on connections between West African rice agricultural practices and rice agriculture that developed in South Carolina, determined that this device, used in West Africa, was at one time literally a hollowed-out tree trunk that was plugged and unplugged at one end to control water flow (Carney 2001). The job of opening and closing trunks, which controlled flooding and draining of rice fields, was extremely

Figure 4.4   Rice trunk in abandoned rice field in South Carolina

important and was done by workers who were called "trunk minders." This was considered a highly skilled job in which precision was highly valued. Trunk minders, primarily men, were responsible for irrigation system management, and the entire yield depended on successful control and management of tidal water flow onto and off of the rice fields. Today this very same irrigation process of trunk minding is done by Park Service personnel at the ACE Basin National Wildlife, which illustrates the importance of making visible African knowledge of irrigation practices on Sea Island rice plantations contained within the historical record.

Rice Production in South Carolina

Soon after its inception in 1670, the colony of Charles Town became known for two things: production of rice and importation of Africans. Africans, primarily from the rice-growing areas along the west coast of Africa, were enslaved and transported directly to Charleston. The largest percentage of Africans in South Carolina and Georgia were acquired from ports of embarkation in Angola, Senegambia, and the windward coast—including Sierra Leone (Littlefield 1991).

It appears that in the Sea Islands, rice was first cultivated in areas of moist soils such as ponds, streams, creeks, and low-lying floodplains requiring no irrigation or controlled flooding of fields. In the early 1700s, soil fertility interests led to inland floodplain swamps becoming the preferred ecosystem for rice production because floodplains were considered extremely fertile (that is, they contained alluvium and decayed swamp vegetation).

By the 1780s, planters began to concentrate almost exclusively on commercial rice production in areas along river swamps, where irrigation technology, through the harnessing of the tidal fluctuations to drain and flood the fields, could be employed (Hilliard 1978; Lees 1980). This was referred to as tidal rice agriculture, and South Carolina became famous for the quality and quantity of rice produced in these fields (Rogers 1970). A map (Figure 4.5) prepared by the National Oceanic and Atmospheric Administration highlights South Atlantic coastal watersheds. It is particularly informative in this discussion because it serves as a template for showing areas along the southeast Atlantic coast where rice production took place. It also serves to underscore places where stories of the transatlantic slave trade and the movement of rice and people between Africa, Europe, the United States, and the Caribbean are a central part of telling America's national story. This relevance of Africans, rice, and slavery to telling a bigger story is authoritatively articulated in the law establishing the Gullah/Geechee Cultural Heritage Corridor as a federally recognized National Heritage Area by the U.S. Congress in 2006.

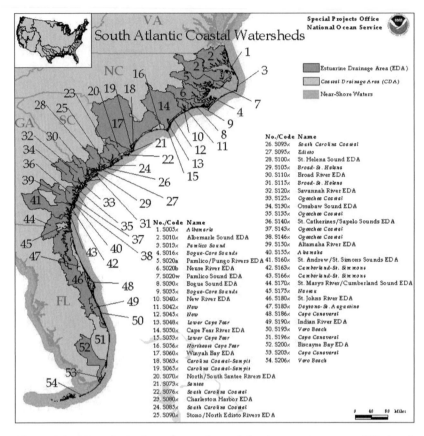

Figure 4.5 Watersheds along the southeast Atlantic coast (courtesy of National Ocean Service, National Oceanic and Atmospheric Administration 1999)

The Gullah/Geechee Cultural Heritage Corridor recognizes the important contributions made by enslaved and free Africans and their descendants to American culture and history. Known collectively as Gullah/Geechee, they labored on antebellum rice plantations in the Sea Islands stretching along the south Atlantic coastal region of the United States (Figure 4.6). Much of the Gullah/Geechee Cultural Heritage Corridor corresponds to areas outlined in the 1999 National Ocean Services Department map. The maps underscore of the relevance and the import of the Gullah/Geechee Cultural Heritage Corridor Commission's mission of providing substantive information about the location of African communities along U.S. Sea Islands and interpreting their presence and contributions—telling a bigger American story.

Figure 4.6   Map of Gullah/Geechee Cultural Heritage Corridor as of 2006 (courtesy of the National Park Service)

During South Carolina's period of commercial rice production, several varieties of rice were cultivated. Judith Carney states that red rice, most likely *O. glaberrima*, was among the first cultivated in South Carolina; however, with the rise of the commercial rice economy and the shift to tidewater cultivation, higher yielding varieties of *O. sativa* were chosen for production and export (Carney 2001). South Carolina rice planter R. F. W. Allston listed four varieties of rice common in the region in an analysis that he prepared for the Agricultural Survey of the State in 1843. These included: (1) the Gold Seed Rice, which he described as "most highly esteemed, and therefore universally cultivated, an oblong grain 3–8ths. of an inch in length, slightly flattened on two sides, of a deep yellow or golden color, awn short; when the husk and inner-coat are removed, the grain presents a beautiful pearly-white appearance" (Allston 1843:4); (2) the Guinea Rice; (3) the Common White Rice; and (4) the White Bearded Rice, which he described as "cultivated more or less extensively by planters for their negroes" (Allston 1843:5). Another planter, John Drayton, in 1802, wrote about rice grown by Africans in South Carolina in this way: "Besides the white and gold rice, already mentioned, there are some others in the State, of little note or consequence; principally cultivated by negros. They are called *Guinea rice*, *bearded rice, a short grained rice*, somewhat like barley, and a species of *highland rice*" (Drayton 1972 [1802]:125; emphasis in the original).

In general, research suggests that Africans in America cultivated a variety of rice types for commercial and personal consumption. The Gullah/Geechee Cultural Heritage Corridor recognizes the significant concentration of African communities along the U.S. Sea Islands and credits their important contributions in telling a bigger American story. The Gullah/Geechee Cultural Heritage Corridor Vision/Mission/Purpose statement as posted on the NPS website reads in part: "The purpose of the Gullah/Geechee Cultural Heritage Corridor is to recognize the important contributions made to American culture and history by African Americans known as the Gullah Geechee who settled in the coastal counties of South Carolina, Georgia, North Carolina, and Florida" (National Park Service website—Gullah/Geechee Cultural Heritage Corridor).

Jehossee—Majority African by Design

Archival Data and Historical Accounts

Census data transcribed for this study provides a snapshot of the demographic make-up of majority African community on Jehossee Island in 1850 and 1860. Information, which was derived from United States Bureau of Census records for St. Johns-Colleton County indicate that 897 enslaved Africans lived on the island by 1850, and 699 lived there in 1860. Age-sex profiles as transcribed and presented for this study (Figure 4.7) offer another means of representing the diversity of the community encountered by visitors to Jehossee Island in 1850 (Jackson 2004). Federal census schedules before 1870 do not list names of persons classified as slaves; however, they do provide age-sex-race markers for enslaved persons. The data graphed in the age-sex-race chart shown in Figure 4.7 serve to provide a further snapshot of African presence on the island—making visible whatever information is contained in the historical record on Africans on Jehossee Island.

Historical accounts of visitors to Jehossee have supplied written documentation of their experiences there, and in some cases, offer glimpses into the daily life and activities of Africans living on the island. Solon Robinson was one such visitor. A well-known writer and agricultural editor for the *American Agriculturist* magazine, Robinson made a series of tours throughout rural America, most extensively between 1840 and 1860, to analyze farming practices of his day and report on agriculture

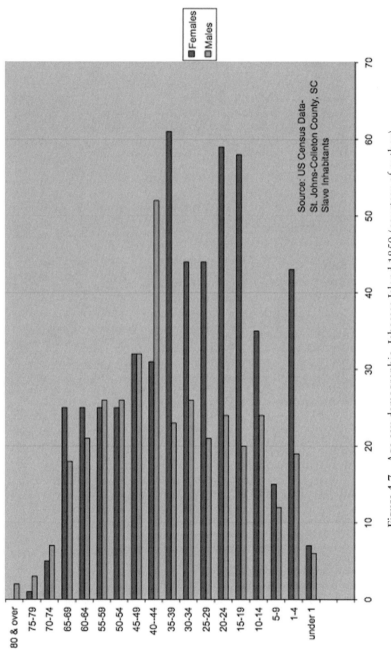

Figure 4.7   Age-sex demographic, Jehossee Island 1850 (courtesy of author)

production operations (Kellar 1936a). After arriving at Jehossee in 1850 by way of a twelve-hour steamboat journey from Charleston (located 30 miles away), Robinson provided the following description of the island in a report that was later published about his findings:

> This island contains about 3,300 acres, no part of which is over ten or fifteen feet above tide, and not more than 200 to 300 acres but what was subject to overflow until diked out by an amount of labor almost inconceivable to be performed by individual enterprise, when we take into account the many miles of navigable canals and smaller ditches. There 1,500 acres of rice lands, divided into convenient compartments for flooding, by substantial banks, and all laid off in beds between ditches 3 feet deep, only 35 feet apart. Part of the land was tide-water marsh, and part of it timber swamp. Besides this, Gov. A. cultivates 500 acres in corn, oats, and potatoes; the balance in gardens, yards, lawns, and in woods, pastures, and unreclaimed swamp.
>
> —Kellar (1936b:364–65)

This description outlines the size of the plantation and underscores the incredible amount of labor required to make and keep the plantation operational. And in his analysis of the plantation's financial status, Robinson explicitly highlights Jehossee's majority African community, identifying the range and type of jobs they performed—clearly placing the responsibility for every aspect of rice production and plantation maintenance throughout the year, even during the "sickly months," in the hands of the majority African community. He writes:

> The average annual sales of the place do not vary materially from $25,000, and the average annual expenses not far from $10,000, of which sum $2,000 is paid the overseer, who is the only white man upon the place, besides the owner, who is always absent during the sickly months of the summer. All the engineers, millers, smiths, carpenters, and sailors are black. A vessel belonging to the island goes twice a week to Charleston, and carries a cargo of 100 casks. The last crop was 1,500 casks—the year before, 1,800, and all provisions and grain required, made upon the place.
>
> —Kellar (1936b:367)

He goes on to state that, according to his estimates, approximately 700 "negroes" lived on Jehossee Island at the time of his visit, and they occupied "84 double frame houses, each containing two tenements of three rooms to a family, besides the cock loft" (Kellar 1936b:367). According to the 1850 census, there were actually 897 enslaved Africans on the island at the time of Robinson's visit, which makes the housing arrangements he describes even more informative of the limited space and extremely cramped conditions in which Africans and their families lived.

For human populations, rice plantation ecosystems present a variety of environmental hazards and stress, the primary problem being malaria. Countless numbers of people in rice plantation environs died from diseases resulting from living and working in conditions of high humidity and standing water—considered prime breeding grounds for mosquitoes. Most planters and their families lived away from their plantations, especially between the months of May and November when malaria was especially prevalent. In contrast, enslaved Africans and their families lived and worked on tidal swamp rice plantations throughout the year.

The magnitude of labor and severity of the toll exacted on the health of those forced to engage in tidal swamp rice production at Jehossee and elsewhere is a reality in which majority African communities in plantation spaces lived. Robinson's observations confirm the intensity of labor demands and the serious threat of sickness for those living and working on the island. Historian William Dusinberre's explicit analysis of the child mortality rate for rice plantation enterprises serves to further temper portrayals of Jehossee as a business enterprise in which the owner's assumed interests in the comfort and happiness of the majority African workforce superseded his/her goal of profiting from their daily labor. Dusinberre writes: "A conservative modern estimate suggests that at least 55 percent of the children born on nineteenth-century rice plantations died by age fifteen" (1996:80). The cause of death was often by enteric and respiratory disease aggravated by medical neglect. In addition, malaria, sunstroke, dysentery, cholera, and other conditions escalated by overwork and the requirements of standing in ankle deep mud and water during periods when the fields were flooded contributed to the high number of deaths among Africans on rice plantations (Carney 2001; Dusinberre 1996).

Nearly sixty years after Solon Robinson's visit to Jehossee Island, noted historian U. B. Phillips visited the island. His visit, which took place around 1907, and subsequent writings provide another look into the life of the majority African community and affirm the continued production of rice on Jehossee into the twentieth century. In a 1918 work, Phillips provided the following brief observation:

> When the present writer visited Jehossee in the harvest season, sixty years after Robinson, the fields were dotted with reapers, wage earners now instead of slaves, but still using sickles on half-acre tasks; and the stack yard was as aswarm with sable men and women carrying sheaves on their heads and chattering as of old in a dialect which a stranger can hardly understand. The ante-bellum hospital and many of the cabins their far-thrown quadruple row were still standing. The site of the residence [Aiken's house], however, was marked only by desolate chimneys,

a live-oak grove and a detached billiard room, once elegant but now ruinous, the one indulgence which this planter permitted himself.

—Phillips (1918:253)

In 1929 he wrote *Life and Labor in the Old South*, which includes two pictures labeled as being taken at Jehossee in the early 1900s. One shows Africans carting sheaves of rice in carts to the stack yard for threshing (1946 [1929]:52), and the other shows the remnant of one of the quarters on Jehossee where African laborers and their families lived (1946 [1929]:164).

Archaeological Accounts

Archaeologically, studies conducted on Jehossee provide yet another perspective on African communities and presence on the island. To date, two formal studies have been conducted. One study was conducted in 1986 by the South Carolina Institute of Archaeology and Anthropology (Charles 1986), and other study was an archaeological and historical investigation of Jehossee Island conducted by the Chicora Foundation, under a contract with the USFWS. It has produced significant information about Jehossee's African community. Research results of this study are documented in published findings authored by Michael Trinkley and team (2002). For example, they identify the following as cultural resources on Jehossee: overseer's summer house, several slave settlements, an African-American cemetery, a rice mill, overseer's house, Aiken main house complex, rice trunk ruins, several rice dike bulkheads, tidal rice mill ruins, and the Brisbane main plantation complex (Trinkley 2002:111). Of particular note is Trinkley's identification of an African-American cemetery and four settlements (and the associated sizes) where Africans on Jehossee lived (Figure 4.8).

Trinkley describes African settlement 38CH1893 as "a large, and somewhat unusually laid out, slave settlement" (2002:116). The site is dated as having been occupied before the Civil War only—with artifacts, including Colono wares found in a range of eighteenth and early to mid-nineteenth century. Colono Ware is described by anthropologist Leland Ferguson as "all low-fired, handbuilt pottery found on colonial sites, whether slave quarters, 'big houses,' or Indian villages" (1992:19). Another African settlement labeled 38CH1897 is described as being among the earliest recorded on Jehossee, occupied before Aiken's ownership with no evidence of occupation into the postbellum period. Artifacts found had a mean ceramic date of 1794, and the artifact assemblage was indicative, according to Trinkley, of a "Freedmen Pattern" (2002:151). Two other African settlements, 38CH1894 and 38CH1895, are described as having nineteenth-century occupation, including into the postbellum period.

SURVEY RESULTS

Introduction

As a result of this reconnaissance level study, 16 sites (38CH1891 through 38CH1906) and one standing architectural site (U/19/2111) were identified on Jehossee Island. Table 11 provides a brief overview of these sites, while their locations are shown in Figure 35 (UTM coordinates have been omitted from this document, but are available on the site forms, recorded with the S.C. Institute of Archaeology and Anthropology).

As discussed in the previous section, all of Jehossee Island was assigned a single archaeological site number, 38CH848, as a result of an earlier reconnaissance level study (Charles et al. 1986). We recommend that this earlier number be disregarded and no longer used in discussions of the island's resources. We have chosen to use a more conventional approach and assign each concentration, or cluster of remains identified during the survey it's own number. This approach allows easier management of the resources. One site has been divided into three loci or areas, although only one number, 38CH1905, was assigned. We believe that this site represents one related dike support system and only one number is therefore appropriate.

We should also briefly mention that this reconnaissance did not attempt to locate, or assign architectural or archaeological numbers, to individual remnant dike systems. There will, however, be some discussion of these features in the summary section, when we consider management and eligibility issues.

Likewise, we did not assign an architectural number to the cemetery, although we did assign such a number to the standing structure. We believe that the cemetery, 38CH1896, is best managed as an archaeological, rather than architectural, resource.

Archaeological Sites

38CH1891

Site 38CH1891 consists of a surface and

Table 11.
Cultural Resources Identified on Jehossee Island

Site Number	Name/Site Type	Size	Eligibility
38CH1891	overseer's summer house	430x50	NE
38CH1892	prehistoric lithic and pottery scatter	130x70	NE
38CH1893	slave settlement	470x430	E
38CH1894	slave settlement	1300x400	E
38CH1895	slave settlement w/postbellum occup	200x1800	E
38CH1896	African American cemetery	350x450	E
38CH1897	rice mill & slave settlement	600x800	E
38CH1898	overseer's house - archaeology	400x300	E
U19/2111	overseer's house - architecture		E
38CH1899	Aiken main house complex	1000x600	E
38CH1900	rice trunk ruins	50x10	NE
38CH1901	rice dike bulkhead	50x900	NE
38CH1902	tidal rice mill ruins	250x250	E
38CH1903	structural remains - possible stable	100x50	PE
38CH1904	footbridge remains	20x100	NE
38CH1905a	rice dike bulkhead	200x25	NE
38CH1905b	rice dike bulkhead	200x25	NE
38CH1905c	rice dike bulkhead	200x25	NE
38CH1906	Brisbane main plantation complex	400x300	PE

Size is in feet
National Register of Historic Places Eligibility: E - eligible, PE - potentially eligible, NE - not eligible

Figure 4.8 Cultural Resources on Jehossee (source: Table 11 in report prepared by Michael Trinkley [2002:111] under contract no. 401812M047 for the U.S. Fish and Wildlife Service)

It is Trinkley's description of site 38CH1896, the cemetery, that is most revealing of African life on Jehossee. In his report (2002:141) he concludes:

Based on the limited information, we believe that this cemetery is intimately associated with the African American presence on the island and, as such, includes burials of both enslaved and free. While its origin is uncertain, a date as early as the first half of the eighteenth century is not unreasonable. Use of the cemetery is not documented beyond 1886, although it may have been used into the first quarter of the twentieth century. By the mid-twentieth century, however, the Jehossee community was broken apart and there were no blacks living on the island.

Trinkley estimates that the cemetery occupies an area of 3.6 acres. He found a total of 200 graves and thinks that the entire cemetery may contain around 1,800 graves.

The findings of Trinkley and team build a vivid profile of the material culture of the community that lived, worked, and died on the island from the eighteenth century through the mid-twentieth century. These archaeological findings highlight the plantation's history of rice production and presence of a large African descendant community on the island.

Jehossee Island in 1995 and 2007—A Personal Accounting

In the fall of 1995, I visited Jehossee for the first time. My visit, 145 years after Solon Robinson's visit and nearly 85 years after Phillips' visit, was to Jehossee Island, now part of the ACE Basin National Wildlife Refuge. I was confronted with tangible reminders of the island as a fully operational rice plantation (Figure 4.9). However, during my most recent visit to Jehossee in 2007, I was once again reminded that my only sources of information about enslaved African people and their connection to rice production on Jehossee Island consisted only of the knowledge being shared with me by the Park Ranger, my own extensive research into the history of the plantation, and a cultural resource inventory done as part of an archaeological study of Jehossee Island (Charles 1986; Trinkley 2002). With respect to the general public, the history and heritage of people who once dominated the space before and after the antebellum period of American history are hidden. The significance of African presence on the island cannot be ascertained from brochures and posters made available to visitors and tourists.

CRITIQUING REPRESENTATIONS

Knowledge about African presence on Jehossee Island has been disproportionately represented as peripheral (subjugated) and rendered invisible. For example, public discussion and knowledge of Jehossee generally revolve around the life, wealth, and social and political prominence of the Aiken family, primarily William Aiken, Jr. (1806–1887). William Aiken, Jr. was a respected planter and well-known political figure, and his father, William Aiken, Sr. was a cotton merchant, businessmen, and planter who immigrated to Charleston from Ireland in 1801. He was active in politics and banking and became one of the wealthiest men in

Figure 4.9 a–b (*Top*) Author at site of slave cabin ruins; (*bottom*) overseer's
house (courtesy of author)

Figure 4.9 c–d (*Top*) Burial marker; (*bottom*) rice mill ruins
(courtesy of author)

South Carolina. Upon his death, William Aiken, Jr. inherited his share of the family's wealth and began to focus his attention on agricultural pursuits, particularly rice. In 1830, he began his acquisition of Jehossee, purchasing a large portion of the land from Thomas Miliken, who had acquired the island from Charles Drayton. It was the Drayton family, owners of the island starting as early as 1776, who initially developed it into a rice plantation (Trinkley 2002). In addition to his ambition as a rice planter, Aiken was also interested in politics. In 1840, he was elected to the State Senate, and in 1844 was he elected Governor of South Carolina. Aiken's reputation as a major producer and exporter of rice coupled with his success in the political arena continually placed Jehossee in public view.

Large-scale commercial rice production on Jehossee ended by the early part of the twentieth century but was revived again in the late 1960s. During this time, rice was once again cultivated—primarily to attract ducks and generate income from duck hunting. Hunters came from all over in pursuit of this and other recreational sport activities. Today, rice grows wild on Jehossee Island, ducks and bird populations are encouraged, and hunting continues as a recreational pursuit. Housed within two National Heritage Areas, possibilities for expanded interpretation of Jehossee Island for presentation to the general public abound.

For example, one of the reasons that I have chosen to privilege the role that Africans played in plantation processes and their role in constructing an important ecosystem is highlighted in a conversation I had with David H. Maybank in 1995. David and his family are former owners of Jehossee Island Plantation. His father, John F. Maybank (who died in 1956), was the son of Harriett Rhett Maybank and grandson of Henrietta Aiken Rhett (William Aiken's daughter). David gave me an oral history of Jehossee Island, including his family's role in developing the island into an important commercial rice enterprise. During our conversation, he also described his experiences as a laborer on Jehossee in the 1950s. At that time, his father was trying to start up rice production operations on Jehossee again. Throughout our discussion he confirmed the significant role that enslaved Africans and their descendants played in the plantation's rice cultivation operations. Indeed, he attributed the plantation's success to their role (David H. Maybank, personal communication, October 1995).

However, what proved most interesting about my conversation with David was his concern about how his family would be represented in future interpretations of the plantation. Since his family had been part of the slave-owning elite, he wanted the story of the significant role that enslaved Africans and their descendants played in building and sustaining the plantation to be told, and at the same time he wanted to protect his family and their reputation in the present. Specifically, he wanted the good that his family did to be put in balance with any critique of slavery and segregation and other systems of oppression that I might construct with respect to enslaved African people and the slaveholding elite for whom they labored. As stated at the start of the chapter, the act of recovery of subjugated knowledge, regardless of the reason, is not benign. I told David that I would tell the story presented in the collected data, and so I have.

Summary

This profile speaks for the enslaved by asking exactly what all those Africans were doing on Jehossee Island rice plantation and other plantations throughout the U.S. South. The answer is especially relevant today, because National Heritage Areas and National Historic sites have been officially sanctioned to tell a story considered to be of national significance about U.S. American history in the public forum.

An active act of heritage resource management includes identifying and critiquing historical representations of antebellum plantation sites that silence or underrepresent the role of enslaved Africans (that is, tourist brochures, online websites, and media stories that focus on sensationalized accounting of plantation slavery, as in the case of many of the Michelle Obama stories). An active act of heritage resource management is a conscious decision to recover knowledge that has been subjugated but that once retrieved can be used to inform and expand public representations of the role of Africans and their descendants in U.S. plantation spaces.

The quest to generate new interpretations of African communities in plantation environments as pursued in this study requires attentiveness to the rigorous and active ways in which dialogues/narratives about plantations as National Heritage sites are constructed and why. Majority African communities living and working on the island engaged in the full spectrum of operations—from field hands, to engineers, to sailors—required to develop and maintain the plantation's 1,500 acres of commercial rice land. Any discussion of Jehossee Island Plantation or the rice ecosystem of the ACE Basin National Wildlife Refuge that fails to mention the history, heritage, and legacy left by the majority African community and their descendants does not erase the reality of their existence but does create tensions around what designations such as National Heritage Area and National Historic Site mean in terms of the presentation of U.S. American history and heritage for future generations.

I specifically advance Scott's theoretical advocacy of a tradition of critical discourse about African peoples in which a "diaspora space" perspective, a broader more encompassing focus, is used to holistically situate and elucidate experiences of African people in plantation spaces. The concept of diaspora space permits the histories of African people in plantation spaces to be interpreted in ways that inform transnational factors affecting change or specific cases of what Eric Wolf (1997 [1982]) calls the global expansion of Europe. This global expansion evoked processes, transformations, and social formations connecting people who developed strategies in response to the circumstance. It is in the context of Jehossee that we can see the story of the Gullah/Geechee Cultural Heritage Corridor and designated communities along the southeast coast from Wilmington, North Carolina, to Jacksonville, Florida, connect with the global movement of rice and people that Judith Carney presents in her book *Black Rice* (2001b) and Edda Fields-Black presents in her book *Deep Roots* (2008). And it is in knowing the story of Jehossee that we can contextualize stories shared by descendants of the enslaved at Friendfield, Snee Farm, and Kingsley plantations. These stories of change in the face of transatlantic slavery unfold and connect across communities, across class, across temporal and spatial boundaries. We become dynamic participants in what David Scott terms the "greathouse debate," about how to read and interpret slavery and the plantation experience anew (Scott 1999). National Heritage Areas are licensed and sanctioned to tell an authorized story of American history and to present it in a public forum. It is in critiquing ways in which knowledge, including stories and histories embodied within entire communities, becomes subjugated that we can expand public presentations of the complexity of American history and heritage within National Historic sites as an active act of heritage resource management.

Chapter 5

"TELL THEM WE WERE NEVER SHARECROPPERS"

The Snee Farm Plantation Community and the Charles Pinckney National Historic Site

MOUNT PLEASANT

Mount Pleasant is an interesting place. The gravesite of a prominent southern white man, John Rutledge, is hidden from plain view in a historically African-American community. According to local stories, John Rutledge, an early American political leader and brother of Edward Rutledge (signer of the Declaration of Independence), is buried in Mount Pleasant, in an unmarked location in the predominantly black community of Phillips.

In Mount Pleasant you find generations of African-descended people still living within walking distance of the plantations on which their great grandparents lived and worked as enslaved laborers. And many descendants of enslaved Africans live and work in the very same communities as their enslaved ancestors did. Community elders share memories of the "plantation bell" ringing long after Emancipation as a call to work and meals throughout the day. Some even receive honorary passes (exemption from entry fees) from local plantations that have now become commercial tourist sites.

A peculiarly southern place, Mount Pleasant reflects social practices of centuries of slavery and segregation in which social interaction between blacks and whites is tempered by complex experiences and ways

Speaking for the Enslaved: Heritage Interpretation at Antebellum Plantation Sites by Antoinette Jackson, 93–112 © 2012 Left Coast Press, Inc. All rights reserved.

of being that are manifested in separateness—in ways of being separate. This dance of knowing your place is particularly evident as a learned means of survival in communities with intimate associations across race, yet with understood boundaries (Jackson 2003).

Mount Pleasant is situated east of the Cooper River just across from the city of Charleston, South Carolina (Figure 5.1). Founded in 1680, Mount Pleasant consists of an incorporated area (the town of Mount Pleasant) and an unincorporated area of historically rural communities and natural spaces. It has a rich and diverse heritage and is an excellent place to view the past and the present in direct relationship. Before 1706, the Seewee Indians populated the area (Derby 1980:15). It is in Mount Pleasant that the famous African art of sweetgrass basketmaking still thrives, and it is in the Mount Pleasant area that the National Park Service (NPS) maintains several historic sites—including Fort Moultrie and the Charles Pinckney National Historic Site.

COMMUNITY DEMOGRAPHICS

Starting around 1721 and until the Civil War, persons of African ancestry constituted an overwhelming majority of the population in the Mt. Pleasant area (Derby 1980; Wood 1974). They labored on local plantations such as Snee Farm, Boone Hall, Laurel Hill, Phillips, and Parkers Island.

A review of the 1790 census of the Charleston District and Christ Church parish region provides a historical demographic snapshot of the community's population (U.S. Census Bureau 1908). Christ Church Parish was one of ten parishes created in the Charleston District by the Church Act of 1706, with Mt. Pleasant coming under the jurisdiction of this parish (Figure 5.2). The 1790 census shows that over 75 percent of the population in the Charleston District were African or African descended as underscored by the population breakdown in Table 5.1 (U.S. Census Bureau 1908:9).

Census records today show that Mount Pleasant has experienced rapid growth as well as a shift in population demographics. Since 1960, the population has grown from 5,000 people to over 47,000 in 2000. Once a historically African majority community, Mount Pleasant, according to year 2000 census figures, is now a community in which African Americans make up less than 10 percent of the population (U.S. Census Bureau 2000).

Long time landowners and residents of Mount Pleasant are feeling the pressure of urban expansion. New housing subdivisions now exist side by side with century old plantation communities (as at Boone

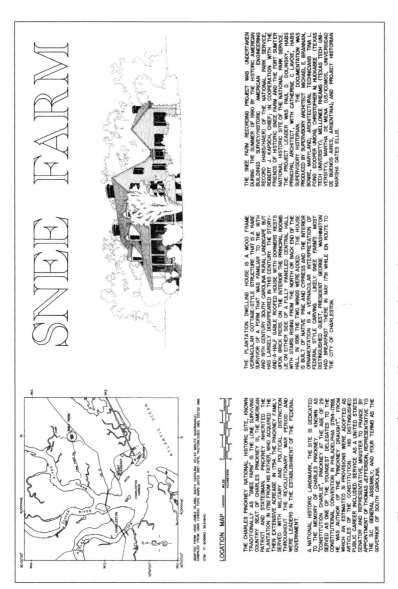

SNEE FARM

LOCATION MAP

ADAPTED FROM USGS JAMES ISLAND, SOUTH CAROLINA 30.4-60 MINUTE QUADRANGLE,
COMPILED FROM USGS 1:24,000 TOPO MAPS DATED 1957-1979, PHOTOREVISED 1983, EDITED 1985
UTM: 17: 609960 / 3634640

THE CHARLES PINCKNEY NATIONAL HISTORIC SITE, KNOWN
TRADITIONALLY AS "SNEE FARM" IS THE LONE SURVIVING
COUNTRY SEAT OF CHARLES PINCKNEY III, THE AMERICAN
PATRIOT AND STATESMAN. PINCKNEY INHERITED THE
PLANTATION IN 1782 FROM HIS FATHER WHO ACQUIRED THE
THEN EXTENSIVE ACREAGE IN 1754. THE PINCKNEY FAMILY
SERVED WITH MILITARY AND POLITICAL DISTINCTION
THROUGHOUT THE REVOLUTIONARY WAR PERIOD AND
WERE LEADERS IN THE ESTABLISHMENT OF THE FEDERAL
GOVERNMENT.

A NATIONAL HISTORIC LANDMARK, THE SITE IS DEDICATED
TO THE MEMORY OF CHARLES PINCKNEY. KNOWN AS
"CONSTITUTION CHARLIE", PINCKNEY AT THE AGE OF 29
SERVED AS ONE OF THE "YOUNGEST DELEGATES TO THE
CONSTITUTIONAL CONVENTION IN PHILADELPHIA (1794-1769).
HE WAS AUTHOR OF THE "PINCKNEY DRAUGHT", FROM
WHICH AN ESTIMATED 31 PROVISIONS WERE ADOPTED AS
ARTICLES OF THE CONSTITUTION. HIS DISTINGUISHED
PUBLIC CAREER INCLUDED SERVICE AS A UNITED STATES
SENATOR AND REPRESENTATIVE, MINISTER TO FRANCE BY
APPOINTMENT OF THOMAS JEFFERSON, REPRESENTATIVE TO
THE S.C. GENERAL ASSEMBLY, AND FOUR TERMS AS THE
GOVERNOR OF SOUTH CAROLINA.

THE PLANTATION DWELLING HOUSE IS A WOOD FRAME
VERNACULAR COTTAGE-STYLE STRUCTURE THAT IS A RARE
SURVIVOR OF A FORM THAT WAS FAMILIAR TO THE 18TH
AND 19TH CENTURY SOUTH CAROLINA RURAL LANDSCAPE BUT
HAS LARGELY DISAPPEARED IN THIS 20TH CENTURY. THE STORY-
AND-A-HALF GABLE ROOFED HOUSE WITH DORMERS RESTS
UPON BRICK PIERS. ON THE INTERIOR THE PRINCIPAL ROOMS
LIE ON EITHER SIDE OF A FULLY PANELED CENTRAL HALL
WITH STAIRS RISING FROM THE NORTH OR BACK END OF THE
HALL. IN 1936 THE TWO WINGS WERE ADDED. THE HOUSE
IS BUILT OF NATIVE PINE AND CYPRESS AND THE INTERIOR
ORNAMENTATION IS A VERNACULAR INTERPRETATION OF
FEDERAL STYLE CARVING. LIKELY SNEE FARM'S MOST
DISTINGUISHED GUEST, PRESIDENT GEORGE WASHINGTON
HAD BREAKFAST THERE IN MAY 1791 WHILE EN ROUTE TO
THE CITY OF CHARLESTON.

THE SNEE FARM RECORDING PROJECT WAS UNDERTAKEN
DURING THE SUMMER OF 1990 BY THE HISTORIC AMERICAN
BUILDINGS SURVEY/HISTORIC AMERICAN ENGINEERING
RECORD (HABS/HAER) OF THE NATIONAL PARK SERVICE,
IN COOPERATION WITH THE
FRIENDS OF HISTORIC SNEE FARM AND THE FORT SUMTER
NATIONAL HISTORIC SITE OF THE NATIONAL PARK SERVICE.
THE PROJECT LEADER WAS PAUL D. DOLINSKY, HABS
PRINCIPAL ARCHITECT, WITH CATHERINE C. LAVOIE, HABS
SUPERVISORY HISTORIAN. THE DOCUMENTATION WAS
PRODUCED BY SUPERVISORY ARCHITECT MICHAEL E. BRANNAN,
BOWIE, MARYLAND; ARCHITECTURAL TECHNICIANS TINA L.
FONG (COOPER UNION), CHRISTOPHER M. HUCKABEE (TEXAS
TECH UNIVERSITY), MELLONEE RHEAMS (TEXAS TECH UNI-
VERSITY), MARTHA DE MENA (US/ICOMOS, UNIVERSIDAD
DE BUENOS AIRES, ARGENTINA), AND PROJECT HISTORIAN
MARSHA OATES ELLIS.

Figure 5.1   Map of Mount Pleasant, South Carolina (source: National Park Service)

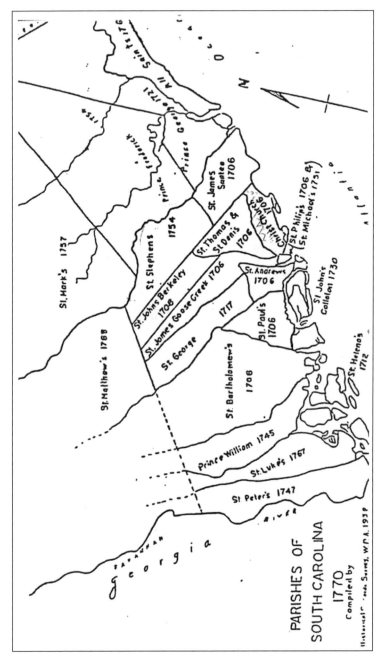

Figure 5.2 Parishes of Charleston District, South Carolina (source: Historical Records Survey W.P.A.)

Table 5.1 Population of Charleston, 1790 (source: U.S. Census Bureau 1908:9)

Population in the Charleston District	
Total	66,985
Enslaved Africans	50,633 (75%)
Population in Christ Church parish	
Total	2,954
Enslaved Africans	2,377 (80%)

Hall, Snee Farm, Phillips, and Snowden). Many of these new subdivisions and businesses are connected in name only to the history of the community (as with Snee Farm Country Club, Brickyard Plantation subdivision, and Sweetgrass shopping center). One African-American community resident shared her perspective on the situation as follows:

> Years ago we could go in those [*sic*] woods. And we go over to those [*sic*] woods now, and they got 2 and 3 million dollar houses back there. You know our people can't even go—one or two can get back there but the majority of us can't go back there for the cost of the houses you know.
> —Scott (2000)

These shifting demographics and community housing patterns described by Ms. Scott are in direct contrast to the relationship that many people living in historically African-American communities have to the area.

AFRICAN-AMERICAN COMMUNITIES, SETTLEMENT PATTERNS, AND LAND OWNERSHIP NARRATIVES

Africans began settling in Mount Pleasant as enslaved plantation workers. Many of the oldest families of Mount Pleasant, including the descendants of enslaved Africans, can be traced to family names listed in the 1790 census report. Today there are several distinct African-American communities in the Mount Pleasant area. Residents whom I interviewed described these historically African communities as extending from the town center of Mount Pleasant to McClellanville—located 25 miles north of Mount Pleasant along highway 17 North. They include, for example, Phillips, Snowden, Six-mile, Tibwin, Seven-mile, Ten-mile, Hamlin, Pineland, and Awendaw. Each community is associated with a major church. Snowden, for example, is associated with Longpoint Baptist Church. Some communities, such as Seven-mile, are named according to their proximity to the town center of Mount Pleasant—this was an important marker historically with respect to access to resources, such as educational facilities.

African Americans established many of these communities following the Civil War as they acquired land and built homes beyond the original plantation boundaries. In a few cases, white families sold land to black farmers (O. D. Hamlin is one example of a land seller), and today many African Americans continue to live and own homes in the Hamlin community.

Elders such as Reverend Harry Palmer shared stories about the history of local communities. For example, Reverend Palmer explained that Phillips is one of the oldest plantation communities in the area, and many of the other communities branched off from it. The Phillips community was at one point part of the Laurel Hill Plantation complex and was given the name Phillips (after a white man from England) to distinguish the location from the rest of the Laurel Hill Plantation. The Phillips community was one of the places set aside for enslaved Africans to live who were not classified as house servants on the local area plantations of Snee Farm, Boone Hall/Brickyard, and Laurel Hill. The Phillips/ Laurel Hill community includes Martin Point (today River Town) and Wagner (today Dunes West) subdivisions and is located off highway 17 on route 41 starting at Joe Rouse Road and extending to the Dunes West subdivision. "After slavery, all the land in Phillips was donated and later deeded to ex-slaves according to family size—with families being given between 2 [and] 12 acres each" (Palmer 2000). The Phillips community was all black until the 1940s. Phillips was home for many of the Snee Farm and Boone Hall Plantation labor force before and after slavery. Today Phillips remains a predominately black community.

Other community residents whom I interviewed were quite proud of their long-term land ownership status. Ms. Gaillard's family, for example, did not do sharecropping but were landowners who worked for wages and also lived on Boone Hall Plantation, because their jobs required them to be in close proximity to the main house. According to family history, Serena Jefferson Linen, Ms. Gaillard's grandmother and a highly acclaimed cook on Boone Hall Plantation, purchased 18 acres of land at 50 cents an acre from plantation owner Major Horlbeck. The money to purchase the land was obtained from an uncle who, she says, had saved his money and buried it under a tree until freedom came (Gaillard 2000). The land that Serena Jefferson Linen purchased still remains in the Gaillard family, and the street where the family house sits today is named Linen Lane. Another community resident, Ms. Scott, a descendant from a family of Mount Pleasant–area basketmakers, stated that: "The average black had their own property. They worked and got paid" (Scott 2000). In the narratives shared by Gaillard and Scott, we see how community residents reflect on relationships between property ownership status and labor. In addition, these stories remind us of the import of recognizing the nuanced ways descendants of enslaved Africans lived their lives and managed their labor and family obligations.

Cultural Preservation in Antebellum Plantation Spaces

This chapter critically examines categorization as an active process of knowledge construction that directly influences ways in which we interpret the past and, more important, create interpretations for future generations. One outcome of reinterpreting the labor practices is that *sharecropper*, as a fixed and universally representative laborer category of descendants of enslaved Africans and one that legitimizes and reinforces notions of dependency, is disrupted. Instead, we find descendants' interpretations of their own work lives and roles as laborers are much broader. However, the sharecropper label is just one example of how categorizations misrepresent how descendants of enslaved Africans understood their occupational statuses in Mount Pleasant. Some narratives also reveal how limited terminology about and limited understanding of labor roles obscure the skilled nature of labor that Africans performed and masks cultural continuity and agency expressed on a family and community level. There was an intergenerational transmission of knowledge about foodways and labor practices that still marks cultural preservation practices in African communities in former antebellum plantation spaces.

Whenever I spoke to long-time African-American residents of Mount Pleasant, they consistently stated: "We were never sharecroppers." After I examined tourist literature, local history accounts, and academic sources, their reasons for contesting the sharecropper label became obvious. In public historical profiles, descendants of enslaved Africans were represented as having progressed along a hierarchy from former slaves to sharecroppers (see Charleston Area Convention and Tourist Bureau website advertisement of a 2008 museum exhibit "From Slave to Sharecropper"). The sharecropper category refers to a farmer who is given credit for seeds, tools, food, housing, and access to land, with part of the harvest going to repay the landowner. This description typically implies that the sharecropper is not a landowner. Such a description fails to recognize the land-ownership status and distinctions in employment patterns of many descendants. For example, this excerpt from a tourist website for the city of Charleston, describing Boone Hall Plantation, still refers to descendants as sharecroppers: "The plantation [Boone Hall] includes a large post-civil-war farmhouse, a number of original slave cabins (which were occupied by sharecroppers well into the twentieth century), several flowering gardens, . . . " (Charleston Private Equity LLC website n.d.).

Indiscriminate use of the term *sharecropper* masks the dynamic ways in which descendants of enslaved Africans interpreted their lives and the wide range of skilled laborer roles that they assumed in plantation communities. By focusing on a single category of labor, the use of *sharecropping*, as universally representative of the scope of work that enslaved Africans and their descendants engaged in, does not acknowledge the breadth of labor practices in antebellum and postbellum plantations. Such limited characterizations reveal how fixed notions of identity within an antebellum plantation narrative create and reproduce narrow representations of enslaved Africans and their descendants, as well as limited interpretive options for public presentations of national history.

The significance of categorization and categorical systems to this discussion is that the value attached to them as forms of knowledge about the past has significant implications in the present (Valentine 2007). The category of sharecropper and the placement of enslaved Africans and their descendants within it actively dictates and influences how we know and remember the past (Connerton 1989; Wilkie 2001). This categorization in turn influences contemporary discourse on descendants of enslaved Africans, slavery, and plantations—particularly evident in the robust discussions that erupted in 2008 when it was revealed that First Lady Michelle Obama was a direct descendant of an enslaved African who lived and worked on Friendfield Plantation in South Carolina.

A Federal Call for Expanded Interpretation

In 1988, the United States Department of Interior authorized the establishment of the Charles Pinckney National Historic Site in Mount Pleasant, South Carolina, for interpreting and representing the life of Charles Pinckney. Pinckney (1757–1824) was a noted drafter of the U.S. Constitution and an outspoken advocate for slavery, who served as a U.S. Senator, member of the House of Representatives, and as a two-term Governor of South Carolina. He fought hard to defend the institution of slavery—arguing for the three-fifths clause (which expanded political representation in the slaveholding states by counting 60 percent of the enslaved African population), the fugitive slave clause, and the continued importation of enslaved Africans into the United States until 1808 (Finkelman 1996). Snee Farm was Pinckney's country retreat as well as a working plantation where slave labor primarily produced rice, cotton, corn, and later pecans. The 1810 census records for Christ Church parish show that Pinckney owned fifty-eight slaves. In 1990, the stated purpose for preserving this site was later expanded to include an interpretation of the life of "all" the site's inhabitants, free and "slave" (Blythe 2000).

According to archaeological findings, the plantation house that Governor Charles Pinckney inherited was constructed around 1754, soon after his father, Colonel Charles Pinckney, purchased the property. Governor Pinckney, who exemplified the life and privilege typical of South Carolina aristocracy at that time, owned Snee Farm from 1782 until 1816. The original house, built during the Pinckney family era of ownership of the plantation, was completely destroyed by fire in the 1820s. The Matthews family, who purchased Snee Farm in 1828, constructed a new "big" house on the property after the original Pinckney house was completely destroyed. This house, which is still standing (Figure 5.3), remained basically unchanged until 1936, when the Ewing family purchased the property and enlarged it (Blythe 2000).

Snee Farm's location along tidal marshes made it highly suitable for growing rice. Although this farm was not comparable in size or level of commercial production to Jehossee Island or Friendfield, the Pinckney and Matthews family are documented as having derived income from its rice production (Williams 1978). An 1840 plat of the Snee Farm Plantation identifies rice land areas among the 915 total acres of the property (Figure 5.4).

Figure 5.3 Snee Farm main house and Charles Pinckney National Historic Site (source: National Park Service)

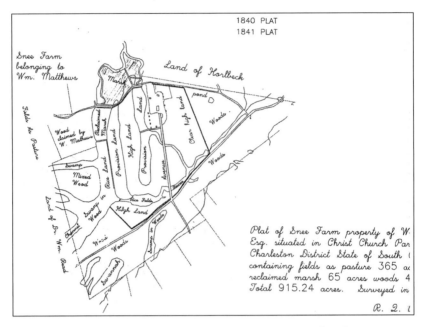

Figure 5.4 Plat of Snee Farm property (source: National Park Service)

Snee Farm has gone from an over 700-acre plantation in full operation to a 28-acre heritage and tourist site (Figure 5.5). It is located adjacent to the Boone Hall Plantation, which is shown as the Land of Horlbeck on the 1840 Matthews plat. The plantations are connected both through their proximity to the Wando River and through family and community associations (Figure 5.6).

Snee Farm was eventually purchased by Thomas J. Hamlin in the 1900s. The Hamlin family maintained control of the plantation until it was purchased by Thomas Ewing and family in the 1930s. During the same period that the Ewings owned Snee Farm, Thomas A. Stone, who was also married to Ewing's daughter, purchased and owned Boone Hall Plantation (1,300 acres). Boone Hall, long known for its excellent brickmaking operations, including its brick slave quarters, as well as its expansive avenue of oaks and large pecan grove, has changed ownership from the Boones to Major John S. Horlbeck to Thomas Stone and today is owned by the McRae family.

A National Park Service project to study African communities formerly associated with Snee Farm Plantation (Charles Pinckney National Historic Site) in Mount Pleasant forms the basis of the analysis in the rest of this chapter. Interview data collected from descendants of enslaved Africans and others associated with Snee Farm and the adjacent Boone Hall Plantation community reveal the scope, complexity, and heterogeneity of African life

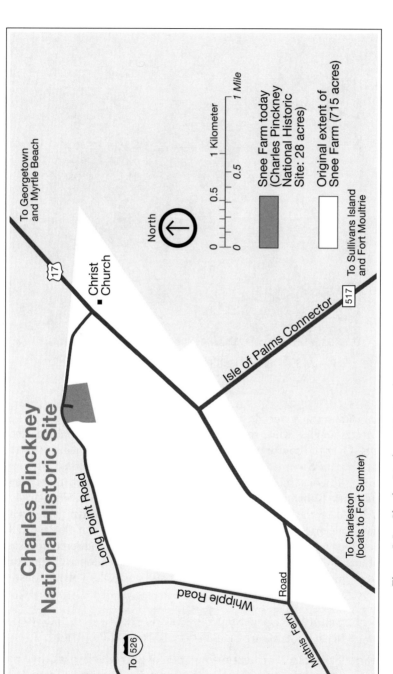

Figure 5.5 Charles Pinckney National Historic Site map (source: National Park Service)

Figure 5.6   Boone Hall Plantation, Horlbeck Creek,
a Wando River tributary (courtesy of author)

in plantation settings outside a *Gone with the Wind* (Mitchell 1936) trope
that depicts an elite white male plantation owner and marginalized black
servants. Over the course of my study I interviewed many members of the
Mount Pleasant community, including painters, cooks, basketmakers, longshoremen, deacons, mothers, sisters, brothers, fathers, preachers, business
owners, Park Rangers, fishermen, quilters, artists, and teachers (Jackson
2003, 2004). In the rest of this chapter, I focus on the Brown family, who
elucidate categories of labor practices broader than those that have typically
been ascribed to descendants of enslaved Africans. Their interpretations can
contribute to shaping future conversations and public dialogue about work
and labor during slavery and on antebellum and postbellum plantations.

ORAL HISTORIES AND DESCENDANT INTERPRETATIONS: RECATEGORIZING
KNOWLEDGE ABOUT PLANTATION LABORING PRACTICES

In the Snee Farm case, a critical examination of the research data collected
shows that the skills and knowledge required to perform occupations
such as those listed in the 1860 U.S. Census table of South Carolina

Occupations were in many cases learned from elders who applied their knowledge during slavery. This knowledge in turn has been transmitted through intergenerational communication and shared with pride as an important family resource, as reflected in the stories people choose to tell and the traditions they choose to continue. People engaged in continuing these labor traditions today are, in many cases, acclaimed as highly skilled artisans and are compensated as such (Lyons 1997; Rosengarten 1986). Information about the history of sweetgrass basketmaking authored by sweetgrass basketmaker and community resident M. Jeannette Gaillard Lee, for example, is featured on the Mount Pleasant Official Town website. It reads, in part: "Sweetgrass basket sewing is viewed as a gift from God. The craft, handed down from generation to generation is usually learned from childhood. Baskets require a great deal of patience and creativity, as there are no set patterns" (2000).

Identifying labor lineages such as expressed by M. Jeannette Gailliard Lee exemplify the problematic nature of situating enslaved Africans and their descendants as sharecroppers. Such simplistic categorizing does not fully reflect the scope of knowledge and the type of work in which people engaged, nor does it speak to the fact that skill transfer was intergenerational.

THE BROWN FAMILY

The Brown family was the last family to live and work on Snee Farm Plantation. They stayed on Snee Farm until 1968, performing work as foremen, laundresses, maids, mechanics, gardeners, millers, nannies, carpenters, and cooks. Table 5.2 provides a snapshot of the tasks performed on Snee Farm Plantation between 1920 and 1968 by the Brown family and other community residents interviewed.

Narrative descriptions shared by the Brown family as well as by other members of the Snee Plantation community help expand static views of jobs and laboring responsibilities that are listed on the 1860 U.S. Census table of South Carolina Occupations and other Census report charts. For example, Mr. Henry Brown (2000), born in 1939, and owner of his own painting business, explained that his grandmother, Cecelia Brown, was the plantation cook and a nanny to the plantation owner's children, as well as a mother and a wife. Mr. Brown's account reveals the differing roles and responsibilities that his grandmother occupied and the breadth of her skill, knowledge, and social responsibilities. Additionally, Peter Brown, another descendant, who was born in 1949, provided the following portrait of his grandmother, Cecelia Brown: "I can see her face right now. She was a very nice lady. She . . . always smoked a pipe, you know, and she was a very strong woman. I loved her very dearly. You

Table 5.2 Snee Farm job occupations (source: Gibbs 2006; Jackson 2004)

Occupation	Person	Description
Gardner	Jesse Ellis, Sr., 1936–37	A local nursery planted gardens. Ellis managed the gardens year 'round.
	Henry Brown	
Foreman	Charlie Stroder,	Supervised the property for the owners and paid the workers.
	Billie Seabrook,	
	Mr. Kinsey	
Firing furnace	Jesse Ellis, Sr.	Fired the furnace with coals.
Head man	Peter Brown	In charge of day-to-day operations of the farm.
	Aaron Smalls	Lived on the farm.
	Ben Doctor	
Cook	Annie Huggins	Prepared all meals.
	Cecelia Brown	
Laundress	Mariah Simmons	Washing and ironing the clothes for the owner and family, 2 days/week.
Maid	Maggie Brown Cooper	Clean the house: dishes, floors, bathrooms.
Wood cutter		Cuts wood for 6 fireplaces, 40 cords per year.
Nanny	Cecelia Brown	Raised O. D. Hamlin, Jr.
Midwife	Alice Smalls	Delivered both black and white babies in the community.
Farm laborers	Henry Brown	Picked pecans, tomatoes, cucumbers, and other vegetables.
	Mattie Galliard	
	Elizabeth Coakley	
	M. Scott	

know she never complained about aches and pains except in later years" (Peter Brown 2000).

And her daughter, Ms. Maggie Brown Cooper, age 85 at time of my visit, had worked on Snee Farm for over fifty years. She was a maid. She remembers that both she and her mom would work from 8 in the morning to 11 at night and that her mom was responsible for cooking three meals a day. She said that her family had worked for the Hamlin, Ewing, and Stone families (personal conversation July 1, 2000). Many women like Mrs. Brown were caretakers for multiple families including their own. Mrs. Brown, who was a wife, mother, and grandmother within in her own family, also had multiple laborer roles and family responsibilities within other households.

According to historical records, Thomas J. Hamlin and Osgood Hamlin owned Snee Farm from 1900 to 1936 (Gibbs 2006), and so members of the Brown family who worked on Snee Farm between 1920 and 1935 were employed by the Hamlin family. The Hamlins are one of the founding families of Mount Pleasant and are listed in the 1790 Census report (Table 5.3). The Hamlin family has a history of securing the labor and services of enslaved Africans and their descendants, such as the Browns, on plantations located throughout Christ Church parish. However, relations between these two antebellum descendant families, the Hamlins and the Browns, have remained congenial; both families have expressed genuine respect and admiration for each other—sharing an identity of "old timers" of the Mount Pleasant community.

When interviewed, O. D. Hamlin II, born in 1915 and raised on Snee Farm Plantation, said of Maggie Brown, also born in 1915 on Snee Farm, that she was one of the "good old people" (Hamlin 2000). Maggie Brown's mother, Mrs. Cecelia Brown, the plantation cook and nanny, "raised" O. D. Hamlin. O. D. said that his grandfather, Thomas Hamlin, purchased Snee Farm in the early 1900s, and following the death of his father (O. D.'s father, Osgood Hamlin I) Snee Farm was sold to the Ewing family, who purchased it in 1936. O. D. and his family then moved to Hamlin Farms—part of Thomas Hamlin Tract originally purchased in 1690—which is where my interview with him took place (Hamlin 2000).

It seems that at one time or another most people interviewed had worked for Hamlin Farms or on a local plantation or indicated that that they were related to someone who had. Informants consistently described truck farming as a major activity (Jackson 2004); however, the overwhelming majority continued to engage in agricultural pursuits. Many provided an inexpensive source of labor on such local plantations as Boone Hall and Snee Farm.

As has been mentioned, the Ewing and Stone families owned Snee Farm during the period 1936–1968. During that time, Henry Brown

Table 5.3 Excerpt of head of families and their slave holdings, Charleston, South Carolina

Head of Family Census Data, Christ Church Parish, 1790

C. Brown	(11 slaves)
John Boon	(40 slaves)
H. Bonneau	(2 slaves)
Gabrial Capers	(82 slaves)
George Capers	(15 slaves)
Andrew Hibben	(29 slaves)
James Hibben	(7 slaves)
William Huggins	(12 slaves)
Eli Huggins	(4 slaves)
Hanner Hamlin	(5 slaves)
William Hamlin	(26 slaves)
Thomas Hamlin	(14 slaves)
Mary Hamlin	(1 slave)
Sarah Rutledge	(64 slaves)
Joseph Wigfall	(83 slaves)
A. Vanderhorst	(117 slaves)
Will Scott	(70 slaves)

Excerpt of Head-of-Family Names, St. Thomas Parish, and Their Slave Holdings, 1790

Marg Bennet	(17 slaves)
Elizabeth Bonneau	(16 slaves)
Arch Brown	(150 slaves)
William Capers	(29 slaves)
Gab Manigault	(210 slaves)
Isaac Parker	(93 slaves)
B. Simmons	(112 slaves)

Excerpt of Head-of-Family Names, St. James Santee and Goose Creek Parishes, and Their Slave Holdings, 1790

John C. Ball	(82 slaves)
John Gaillard	(115 slaves)
Cha Gaillard	(34 slaves)
Ed Jerman	(73 slaves)
Geo Parker	(48 slaves)
Hugh Swinton	(22 slaves)
Cha Glover	(44 slaves)
Joseph Glover	(123 slaves)

Source: 1790 Census, First Census of the United States

worked on Snee Farm as a caretaker for the garden. His duties included raking leaves, planting flowers, picking pecans, and milking the cows. Henry Brown said that he could pick 200–300 pounds of pecans in one day. And, for his labor he received about a dollar a day, which was paid to him by the foreman on Fridays (Brown 2000).

In addition to the Browns, other members of the community, for example, Jesse Ellis, Sr., age 85, shared accounts of working on Snee Farm. Jesse Ellis worked on the plantation for the Ewing family for two years starting in 1936. He managed the furnace and took care of the flower garden—he was quite proud of his knowledge of the plants and flowers on Snee Farm. After Snee Farm, Jesse worked on Boone Hall plantation for a while; then he went to work at the shipyard, where he stayed for thirty-three years (Ellis 2000).

LIVING IN COMMUNITY

When I look at the collected narratives, one profile that emerges is the significance of elders and grandparents within the community. Many community members interviewed indicated that they had been "raised-up" by a grandparent, particularly their grandmothers. For the most part, community members interviewed did not readily volunteer information about the period they simply referred to as "slavery time." When discussing an event connected to this period, interviewees used the typical beginning and ending statement "that happened during slavery time," and the conversation moved on. Sometimes more information would be shared if a specific question about a kinship relationship or an significant event were asked. For example, questions such as "What did your grandmother's mother do in terms of work?" or "Where did she live?" or "Could she cook?" usually evoked the most direct and enthusiastic responses. Take, for example, the following stories:

> Those real old people, I still believe they had something . . . . that came from Africa . . . . You know, we used to call them old people backwards; we didn't know what they do and they was people of . . . stock. They knew what was goin on and you can believe that.
>
> —Joe Smalls (2000), age 75

> "No Manners" meant you didn't speak to or respect your elders.
>
> You could get your behind "cut" for this.
>
> The old folks trained them right.
>
> —Nathaniel Nelson (2000), age 56

Others shared the following stories about their observations of community connectedness:

Everybody had knowed everybody on Phillips. Everybody was everybody children's parents. That's just the way it was and, uh, even the smallest child as soon as they get large enough, everybody knowed each other.

—Harry Palmer (2000), age 70

People in the area had either a plum, apple, and/or pear tree(s). And a few people had grapevines. Then people traded and shared with one another. There was not much store buying, but people traded and shared with one another. Everybody had a cast net . . . a poor man net, a net that could be used to catch shrimp or mullet. Every family knitted or had their own net. People in the community were lovin' people.

—Joe Smalls (2000)

He [my husband] was a fisherman. He used to fish and give away most of his catch. People didn't really have money, and so just shared what they had.

—Elizabeth Coakley (2000), age 73

Even though plantation owners demarcated plantations by name and land titles, Africans and African Americans generally established communities that extended across plantation lines. Thus talking about Snee Farm in isolation from other plantations in the area proved to be inconsistent with the way in which residents positioned themselves within their communities (Jackson 2003). In addition to articulating the fluidity of labor roles, these narratives also reveal the value of kinship and community. Descendants of the Browns and the Galliards, for example, indicated that they considered all the plantations in the local area as connected and thus related to one another. These stories, articulated by descendants of enslaved Africans living in postbellum plantation spaces, underscore the power of knowledge shared by descendants.

CONCLUSION

In the concluding chapter of their book *The Birth of African-American Culture* (1992 [1976]), Mintz and Price suggest research directions for examining contemporary African-American society in light of the transatlantic slave trade. These include ethnographic procedures as well as historically focused analysis. However, few studies focus on African communities in plantation spaces and challenge static characterizations of plantation life at designated National Heritage sites in the United States from a cultural anthropological perspective. In this chapter, I focused on transatlantic slavery, plantation life, descendant interpretations, and ways in which descendant memories instruct reconfiguration of systems of categorizations.

Descendants of enslaved people help in reinterpreting plantation spaces—specifically, systems of categorization and the meanings of categories that narrowly define home, family, community, labor, and landownership practices. Their stories, observations, and lived experiences have often been misrepresented or underrepresented at public heritage sites, in media representations, and by scholars. Descendants consulted in this analysis, such as Ms. Gaillard, Ms. Scott, Reverend Palmer, and the Brown family, shed light on broader dynamics for characterizing plantations to include family, community, and the effects of global and historical processes. They contribute to the formulation of a rubric of knowledge that sidesteps the solidifying effects of fixed categorizations (see also the critique of the solidifying effects of binarism in Boellstorff 2005); this is the case specifically in the areas of landowner and laborer roles. If one focuses on how descendants articulate both their and their ancestors' laborer and landowner statuses, new ways of presenting plantations emerge.

African Americans in Mount Pleasant engaged in a variety of subsistence and commercial activities immediately following the Civil War. By examining the dynamics operating within the context of this community, the issue of sharecropper as a universally representative status can be reinterpreted in several ways. One way is to critically examine how hierarchal classifications of agricultural labor such as landowner, tenant, sharecropper, and wageworker are defined and recognized in census reporting and other statistics. In these classification schemes, landowner is recognized at the top level, and wageworker is defined as the lowest category (Alston and Kauffman 1998). The rigidity embedded in the application of this classification system neither accounts for nor accurately represents the multiplicity of labor roles in which African Americans in Mount Pleasant engaged. Instead, it fixes people in one category or another, misrepresenting the complexity and fluidity of the lives led. In Mount Pleasant, many descendants of enslaved African people simultaneously occupied multiple categories on the agricultural labor scale—for example, those of landowner and wageworker. It was explained that during the week or for extended periods of time, wageworkers sometimes stayed on the plantations or farms where they labored. People also reported that they returned to their own land and homes on their days off or for specific social and community activities, such as religious services on Sunday. Community residents interviewed therefore consider the fact that they own their own land a critical aspect of their social identity as opposed to their varying labor roles and employment pursuits. By interpreting the fluidity of roles that people occupy in the way they have chosen to talk about, differentiate, and value themselves, one highlights the scope, variety, and complexity of laboring practices, family responsibilities, and cross-plantation connections in Mount Pleasant, South Carolina. More important, it offers another way of thinking about slavery and plantation life beyond the staid representations of dependency, shame, and exploitation. Although these representations are not incorrect, they are incomplete and do little to provide an understanding of the ways in which enslaved Africans and their descendants were skilled, created community, exerted agency, and navigated the complexities and challenges in antebellum and postbellum plantation spaces and environments.

Although the sharecropper label has been uniformly ascribed to descendants of enslaved Africans in public accounts of Mount Pleasant plantation community history, the oral histories of African-American descendants of the community detailed in this chapter help counter such portrayals. Their representations of the past underscore the importance of utilizing more complex models of interaction and interpretation, which can elaborate, and not obscure, the variety and fluidity of roles (that is, landowner, tenant, wage laborer, mother, father, grandparent, caretaker) that Africans and their descendants performed in plantation communities.

This approach to recovering/reframing how knowledge is categorized is transformative, because it models a process for critiquing representations—in this discussion, a process for critiquing representations of enslaved Africans and their descendants, particularly with respect to fixed ideas about plantation labor practices and today's associated socialcultural and economic implications. It documents ways of making visible a breadth of labor activities pre- and post-emancipation that have often been overlooked by other interpretative traditions and approaches. This is especially evident in presentations that focus solely on the "big house" perspective for public displays of national heritage.

My work and the analyses presented in this chapter incorporate descendant narratives of the enslaved in the context of specific families and communities and are posited as methodological interventions aimed at assessing the impact of systems categorization and at making the research and interpretation of plantation spaces an ongoing process. I argue that this approach shatters universally applied labels (that is, labor-related labels) and unfetters descendants from binarism in labor and landowning statuses stemming from rigid categorization systems. It also expands notions of plantation spaces as geographically bound. The Kingsley Plantation community discussion that follows offers a way of thinking about postbellum communities in global context from a diaspora perspective—beyond geographic, spatial, social, and temporal boundaries. It shows how expanding ways of thinking about plantation spaces collapses categories, blurs lines, and disrupts demarcations that act to segregate communities, families, and people.

Chapter 6

THE KINGSLEY PLANTATION COMMUNITY

A Multiracial and Multinational Profile of American Heritage

When Kingsley descendant Manuel Lebrón spoke with me on November 8, 2010, he emphasized this phrase: "The Kingsleys travel around a lot." It was his family's mantra. And after listening to his story, I can say it appears to be as true now as it was for his great-grandparents, Zephaniah and Anna Kingsley, back in the 1800s. Manuel, a seventh-generation Kingsley descendant through his mother's kinship line, is a U.S. citizen from the Dominican Republic. He was born a Spanish citizen (his father is from Barcelona, Spain) but grew up and attended school in the Santo Domingo area of the Dominican Republic (DR), which is where his mother's family originates. He graduated from the Parsons School of Design in New York City, moved to Barcelona in 2006, and worked as a graphic designer for the nongovernmental organization. Oxfam in Europe. Most recently he was accepted into the national Teacher Training program in England and was living in London. He says he is often reminded of Zephaniah Kingsley and is obsessed with learning as much as possible about the history of his family.

The life and business activities of Zephaniah Kingsley, Jr., born in Bristol, England in 1765, and Anta Majigeen Ndiaye (Anna Kingsley), born in Senegal, West Africa in 1793, who Kingsley purchased, fathered children by, and established households and businesses with in Florida and Haiti, underscore the reality of the transatlantic slave trade. The Kingsley's multiracial, multinational family and their connections, associations, and relationships with people and communities on local and global levels provide insight into the transition and movement of African descendant people within and outside plantation landscapes in the Americas.

By focusing on the scope of heterogeneous relationships that linked Africans and Europeans beyond fixed social, spatial, and temporal contexts, a diaspora space perspective enables reimagining plantations to include a broader more complex scope of experiences (Jackson 2009). In this chapter, I introduce Manuel Lebrón and his kinship connection with Anna and Zephaniah Kingsley to show how the African diaspora experience is intertwined with the everyday lives of people and the spaces in which they interact. This analysis is anchored by two time periods. One period focuses on Zephaniah Kingsley's arrival in Florida around 1803 through his purchase of various plantation sites, including what is now the Kingsley Plantation site. The other period captures the present, in which oral history and interview testimony conveyed by descendants and local area residents help frame the plantation community today.

THE KINGSLEY LEGACY

Zephaniah Kingsley was a wealthy planter, businessman, and trader. His father was an English Quaker, and his mother was of Scottish descent. He lived a life of constant migration. In 1793, Kingsley took an "oath of naturalization" in Charleston, South Carolina. In 1798, he took an "oath of loyalty" to Denmark while employed as a ship captain on the island of St. Thomas, and then in 1803, he took a third "oath of loyalty," as a Spanish citizen of Saint Augustine, East Florida (Schafer 2000). He owned and captained ships and was actively involved in the transport of Africans between Africa, the Caribbean, and the Americas.

Between 1802 and 1808, for example, Zephaniah Kingsley specifically imported Africans into Florida, Georgia, and South Carolina for his own plantation interests. A shipping document from the year 1802 lists Kingsley as the first captain of a ship called *Superior*, which arrived at the Port of Havana with 250 Africans. Obtained from unspecified regions in Africa, they were sold into slavery in the Americas under the direction and discretion of Zephaniah Kingsley (Eltis et al. 1999). The following entry provides example of Kingsley's introduction of Africans into a province in Florida:

> Certified and sworn that Zephaniah Kingsley introduced into the province, 64 slaves; 21 of them in the sloop "Laurel" from the port of San Tomas, 5/5/1804; 10 on 6/25 of the same year in the schooner "Laurel," alias the "Juanita", proceeding from Havana; 16 in the sloop "El Jefe,"

coming from Charleston, 7/15/1806; 3 in the schooner "Esther," coming from Havana, on 10/21/1806; and 10 in the schooner "Industria," coming from Georgia, 3/9/1808. Signed: Entralgo, St. Augustine, 1/27/1814.

—Spanish Land Grants (1941:21)

The central theme of the Zephaniah Kingsley story is his acknowledged spousal relationship with Anta Majigeen Ndiaye, a West-African woman described as being of royal lineage from the country of Senegal (Corse 1931; Glover 1970; May 1945; Schafer 1996; Stephens 1978). Anta (Anna Kingsley) is thought to be one of three *bozales* (*bozal* = newly imported person from Africa) whom he purchased and transported from Havana, Cuba, to Florida in 1806 (Schafer 1996). The following entry describes the arrival of the three *bozales*:

In 1806, a ship by the name of Esther, Captained by Henry Wright, acquired cargo in the Port of Havana, Cuba, and set sail for South Carolina. Listed among the "cargo," per the order of Zephaniah Kingsley, were "Tres Negras bozales piezas á trescientos . . . 300 p . . ." ["Three female Negroes freshly arrived from Africa at a price of 300 p' each"]. The cargo was registered to Spencer Man of Charleston, South Carolina, a passenger onboard the ship along with Zephaniah Kingsley. However, en route to its intended destination, the ship was detained in St. Augustine, Florida, where the cargo was unloaded and released to the possession of Zephaniah Kingsley.

—East Florida Papers

According to Zephaniah's own accounts, he married Anna in accordance with her native customs and established a home with her at his plantations in East Florida (that is, Laurel Grove and Kingsley Plantation) and later in Haiti. He had four children with her: George, Mary, Martha, and John (Table 6.1). He is said to have acknowledged and provided for them, and his July 1843 will, although heavily contested by Martha Kingsley McNeill (Zephaniah's sister), attests to this. Anna Kingsley is also recorded as having owned enslaved Africans herself, and many accounts of the Zephaniah story underscore this. In addition to Anna, Zephaniah Kingsley maintained relations with a number of other African women and acknowledged paternity for the children he fathered with them.

Around 1837, Kingsley sold most of his Florida property and resettled his extended family in Haiti. Schafer writes that:

He sold most of his Florida properties and purchased several plantation tracts in the free black Republic of Haiti, where Anna Kingsley and her sons George and John Maxwell, along with other Kingsley co-wives and children and fifty slaves, settled in 1837. Kingsley urged two daughters

Table 6.1 Kingsley family descent chart

---

1. Zephaniah Kingsley, Sr. sp: Isabella Johnstone
    2. **Zephaniah Kingsley, Jr.** (b. 1765 d. 1843) sp: **Anna (Anta Majigeen) Ndiaye** (b. 1793 d. 1870)
        3. George Kingsley (b. 1807) sp: Anatoile Francoise VaunTravers (m. 1849)
        3. Martha Kingsley Baxter (b. 1809) sp: Cran (? Oran) Baxter
        3. Mary Elizabeth Kingsley (b. 1811) sp: John S. Sammis
            4. Egbert Kingsley-Sammis
            4. George Kingsley-Sammis
            4. Edmund Kingsley-Sammis sp: ? Lizzy
        3. John Maxwell Kingsley (b. 1824)
    2. Mary Kingsley-Charlton (b. 1764)
    2. Johnstone Kingsley (b. 1767)
    2. George Kingsley (b. 1768)
    2. Catherine Kingsley-Bardon (b. 1770)
    2. Elizabeth Kingsley (b. 1772)
    2. **Isabella Kingsley Gibbs** (b. 1774) sp: **George Gibbs III**
        3. Kingsley Beatty Gibbs
        3. Zephaniah C. Gibbs
        3. George Couper Gibbs 2nd
        3. Sophia M. Gibbs
        3. Isabella M. Gibbs
        3. George Kingsley Gibbs
        3. Isabella J. Gibbs
    2. **Martha Kingsley McNeill** (b. 1775 d. 1852) sp: **Daniel McNeill**
        3. Charles James Kingsley McNeill
        3. Anna Matilda Kingsley McNeill Whistler, 2nd wife (1808–1881) sp: Maj. George Washington Whistler
            4. James Abbot Kingsley-McNeill Whistler
            4. William Whistler sp: Ida Florida Gibbs King (1st wife)
            4. Charles Whistler
        3. Isabella Kingsley McNeill sp: George Fairfax
            4. Adm. Fairfax
        3. Catherine Kingsley McNeill sp: Dr. George Palmer
        3. Mary Kingsley McNeill sp: Joseph Estabrook
        3. Gen. William Gibbs Kingsley McNeill sp: Maria Commnons

---

Source: Gibbs family memoirs; sp = spouse

who remained in Florida (both were married to prominent white men) to emigrate to "some land of liberty and equal rights, where the conditions of society are governed by some law less absurd then that of color."

—Schafer (2000:113)

Schafer, a historian whose research has led him to determine that Anna was probably one of the three Africans whom Zephaniah purchased and transported onboard the *Esther* to St. Augustine in October 1806, has described Zephaniah's initial encounter with Anna: "On the September day that Anta was exhibited for sale, a merchant from Spanish East Florida mingled amidst the crowd of buyers. A slaver himself and the owner of a Florida plantation, Zephaniah Kingsley, Jr., noticed the tall Wolof girl with shiny black skin among hundreds of Africans for sale. Kingsley was high bidder that day, purchasing Anta Majigeen Ndiaye and two other African females" (Schafer 1996:134).

And, in an interview with Lydia Child in New York in 1842, Zephaniah Kingsley provides a frank assessment of his slave-trading business activities:

LC: "Then you have been on the coast of Africa?"

ZK: "Yes, ma'am; I carried on the slave trade for several years."

LC: "You announce that fact very coolly," said I. "Do you know that, in New England, men look upon a slave-trader with as much horror as they upon a pirate?"

ZK: "Yes; and I am glad of it. They will look upon a slaveholder just so, by and by. Slave trading was a very respectable business when I was young. The first merchants in England and America were engaged in it. Some people hide things which they think other people don't like. I never conceal anything."

—Lydia Child in Stowell (2000:109) 1844:155–56

Although Kingsley's actions were not unique, he was outspoken in espousing his views and advocating his way of life. He had a vested interest in maintaining slavery as a form of labor for his plantation operations, while at the same time, he advocated for peaceful relations between whites and free "colored" populations as a means of control and protection against revolt. For example, in his "Address to the Legislative Council of Florida on the Subject of Its Colored Population," delivered in 1823, Zephaniah petitioned as follows:

A certain portion or extent of country situated on the Seaboard of the Southern States who's climate is unfavorable to the health and production of white people, seems destined by nature to be cultivated and brought into production and into perfective value by the labor of colored people; of all this portion of territory, extending from the cape of Virginia, southerly to the cape of Florida on the Atlantic coast, and perhaps 100 miles back upon an average from the sea, Florida is by far the most valuable. . . .

In short consider that our personal safety, as well as the permanent condition of our slave property is immediately connected with, and depends upon, our good policy in making it the interest of our free colored population to be attached to good order and have a friendly feeling towards the white population.

—Zephaniah Kingsley (1823)

Zephaniah and Anna Kingsley are central figures in the development of portrayals of the diaspora experiences of enslaved Africans and their descendants connected to the slave trade. For example, I would argue that Anna, purchased in 1806 at the age of 13 by Zephaniah Kingsley, Jr., learned to understand power and how it operated at a young age as his mistress. She managed to secure her freedom and the freedom of her children five years after arriving in Florida. In 1811, Zephaniah signed her emancipation papers, and she became a free woman of color. She went on to successfully run his varied businesses, travel, manage his households in Florida and the Dominican Republic (which as that time was part of Haiti), and enjoy land ownership and wealth herself, including owning enslaved Africans (Schafer 2003). Anna consciously used her knowledge, her beauty, and her position as mistress of the big house (although she lived in the kitchen house) to secure a future for her and her children. She lived and survived in her own way, far from her West-African birthplace of Senegal, leaving precious treasures, children and grandchildren, who have gone on to navigate their own roles and relationships, and culture and identity politics, as Africans in America in plantation communities and elsewhere.

Kingsley Heritage Celebration 2005

In 2005, Manuel Lebrón gave the keynote address at the 8th Annual Kingsley Heritage Celebration held at Kingsley Plantation Site, Jacksonville, Florida, where he spoke of his connection to Anna and Zephaniah Kingsley (Figure 6.1). The title of his talk, *Seeking the Inner Zephaniah—a Descendant's Perspective*, underscored his desire to see his life, his movement, from Santo Domingo to New York City to Barcelona and now London from Zephaniah's perspective (Lebrón 2005).

The Kingsley Heritage Celebration began in 1998 as a result of Lebrón making contact with the National Park Service at the Timucuan Ecological and Historic Preserve site, where the plantation is located. During our

Figure 6.1 Kingsley descendant Manuel Lebrón, keynote speaker, Kingsley Heritage Celebration, October 15, 2005 (source: Lebrón 2005; personal correspondence, November 8, 2010)

conversation, Lebrón said that his father was an airline pilot, and the family was always traveling back and forth between the Dominican Republic and Florida. His excitement was fueled by a 1992 trip to the United States from the Dominican Republic. Although his family always knew that the Kingsley house and parts of the plantation had been preserved, they had never visited. During that trip he saw a brochure about Kingsley Plantation in the Miami airport. At that time he was 15 or 16 years old. After seeing the brochure he contacted Park Service personnel at the Kingsley site, and his initial contact and subsequent conversations led to an internship there. While perusing historical documents as part of his internship in 1997, Manuel suggested to the park personnel that something be done to recognize the 200th anniversary of the construction of Kingsley's house, built in 1798. He also suggested that the celebration honor those who had lived and worked at the site, such as Zephaniah and Anna Kingsley. This led the National Park Service to organize the 1998 Heritage Celebration and Homecoming event (Lebrón 2005; personal communication, November 8, 2010).

The stated goal of the Kingsley Heritage Celebration is to help the local community explore cultural traditions found in modern American society that originated during the plantation period. A Timucuan Preserve/Kingsley Plantation news release dated October 25, 2010, provides this descriptive of the event and the plantation:

> Kingsley Plantation, the location of the event, is a unit of the National Park Service's Timucuan Ecological and Historic Preserve in Jacksonville, Florida. It is named for Zephaniah Kingsley (and his African wife, Anna), who owned and operated a 1,000-acre plantation during the first half of the nineteenth century. In addition to the scheduled events, visitors can tour the grounds, which include Florida's oldest standing plantation house, kitchen building, and barn. The remains of 25 slave cabins offer perhaps the most graphic evidence of slave living quarters and daily life experiences in the state, if not the South.
>
> —National Park Service Timucuan Preserve/Kingsley Plantation website
> news release, October 25, 2010

The Kingsley Plantation Heritage Festival and Family Reunion held in 1998, the first such event at the site, brought together members of the Kingsley Plantation family from as far away as the Dominican Republic and as close as St. Augustine and Jacksonville, Florida. Interviews with many of the reunion participants were conducted and videotaped by University of Florida graduate students, per a request to document the event by the National Park Service Timucuan Ecological and Historic Preserve office. The stories that participants shared provide insight into issues of race and the legacy of slavery as experienced by Kingsley descendants (Jackson 2009).

For example, the Kingsley family inheritance dispute was a topic of discussion for some descendants attending the festival. The dispute centered on a fight for control of Zephaniah Kingsley's estate upon his death in 1843 and was initiated by a lawsuit filed by European descendant family members, most notably Zephaniah's sister, Martha Kingsley-McNeill (May 1945). Family members on this side sued to prevent Zephaniah's African descendant family members, primarily Anna and her children, from receiving their share of the estate, as dictated per the terms of Zephaniah Kingsley's will. The legal battle to revoke the terms of the will lasted several years before the original terms of the will were finally upheld, and Anna Kingsley and her family were allowed to claim their share of the estate. However, by that time, administration costs and legal fees had depleted much of the estate.

William Tucker Gibbs, a sixth-generation European-identified Kingsley descendant of the Isabella Kingsley-Gibbs family line (Table 6.2), described his memory of the dispute when he was interviewed at the festival in 1998:

> And Kingsley was a strange guy who had a lot of money and owned a lot of land and that's ok. He had a lot of power, so they didn't mess with him. When he died, they certainly messed with Anna. I understand that she spent the last years of her life in court more than anywhere else—just trying to keep her property for her children and keep her money. And of course, a black woman—whether you are free or not—your patron—your husband died and he's the guy who's always protected you—you can have all the land, all the money you want, but the powers that be don't want a black woman—think about this—she was a black woman. Not even a black man. They wouldn't want a black man having this kind of power. Can you imagine how they felt about a black woman having all this money and all this land? Hell no [laugher]. So, it's fascinating. It really is.
>
> —William Tucker Gibbs (1998)

At the Kingsley Heritage Celebration, Manuel Lebrón (1998) and his mother Sandra Lebrón stressed the unity of the family and a desire and willingness to personally forget negative aspects of the past and concentrate on establishing positive relationships going forward. Sandra and Manuel trace their connection to the Kingsley family through John Maxwell, a son of Zephaniah and Anna Kingsley (Table 6.3), who established his home in Haiti—in the area that now is the Dominican Republic (Sandra Lebrón 1998).

Narratives shared by other Kingsley descendants further contextualize, and in many instances critically assess, the Kingsley legacy. For example, Peri Frances Betsch, an African-American-identified eighth-generation descendant of Anna and Zephaniah (Table 6.3), shared the following ideas and feelings regarding the circumstances of her great grandmother's (Anna) arrival in Florida and the initial encounter between Anna and Zephaniah,

> Sometimes it makes me laugh.

> But I don't think it was like some . . . "I saw him across the crowded slave market, and he winked at me," that's ludicrous. I can't buy into that. And also you got to think like I would imagine, these people looked crazy to her, like who are you?

Table 6.2   Kingsley-Gibbs descent chart

1. George Gibbs III sp: Isabella Kingsley Gibbs (b. 1774 d. 1837)
    2. **George Couper Gibbs 2nd** (b. 1822 d. 1873) sp: **Julia E. Williams** (2nd wife) / Elizabeth Elcan, 1st wife (1829–1896)
        3. Elizabeth Elcan* Gibbs (b. 1848) sp: John T. Dismukes
        3. George William Gibbs (b. 1853 d. 1923) sp: Margaret Watkins Gibbs (b. 1855 d. 1935)
            4. George Couper Gibbs 2nd sp: Leonora Warnock
                5. Margaret Gibbs sp: ?? Worthington
                    6. Patsy Gibbs Worthington
                    6. William Gibbs Worthington
                5. **Harriet Gibbs Gardiner** sp: ?? Gardiner
                    6. Phillip Gibbs Gardiner
                    6. Stephen Gibbs Gardiner
                    6. Couper Gibbs Gardiner
                5. William Gibbs sp: unknown
                    6. Leonora Gibbs
                    6. **William Tucker Gibbs**
                    6. **Becky Gibbs**
                    6. **Emily Gibbs**
                    6. Denny Gibbs
            4. George William Gibbs 2nd sp: Kathleen M. Ingraham
                5. George W. Gibbs 3rd sp: ??
                    6. **George W. Gibbs 4th**
                    6. Robert Gibbs
                5. Maria Gibbs
            4. Elizabeth Lightfoot Coles Gibbs Weed sp: Joseph Dunning Weed (m. 1911)
            4. Margaret Watkins Gibbs Watt sp: Rev. Albert W. J. Watt
            4. Tucker Carrington Gibbs (b. 1889) sp: Clarissa Anderson Dimick
            4. Rebecca Gibbs Moore (b. 1881) sp: Samuel Moore
        3. Isabella Barksdale Gibbs (b. 1857) sp: Charles Floyd Hopkins (b. 1853 d. 1948)
        3. Robert Kingsley Gibbs (b. 1869 d. 1905)
    2. Kingsley Beatty Gibbs (b. 1810 d. 1859) sp: Laura Matilda Williams (b. 1820 d. 1893)
    2. Sophia M. Gibbs
    2. Isabella M. Gibbs sp: Ralph King

(Continued)

Table 6.2 (*Continued*)

2. Zephaniah C. Gibbs
2. George Kingsley Gibbs
2. Isabella J. Gibbs

Source: The Kingsley Family Genealogy Sources: The Kingsley-Gibbs family memoirs compiled by Margaret Gibbs Watts entitled, "The Gibbs Family of Long Ago and Near at Hand 1337–1967", on file at the St. Augustine Historical Society in St. Augustine, Florida, is a valuable source of information on Kingsley family genealogy.
Probate Records on file at the Duval County Courthouse, Jacksonville, Florida: Martha B. Baxter, Probate Record No. 143 (May 14, 1870); Zephaniah Kingsley, Probate No. 1203 (September 25, 1843); Anna M. Kingsley, Probate Record No. 1210 (June 18, 1870); George Kingsley, Probate Record No. 1205 (December 21, 1846); Stephen Kingsley, Probate 1252 (June 19, 1897); John S. Sammis, Probate No. 1970 (February 26, 1884); Mary K. Sammis, Probate No. 2029 (April 25, 1895).

> I imagine some redheaded white guy with a beard, wearing funny woolen clothing, and she must have been like . . . "You want me to do what?" I just can't picture it. But I really always wonder what was she thinking.
> —Peri Frances Betsch (2001)

Peri Frances is on a personal mission to find out more about her family's ancestral connection to Anna Majigeen Ndiaye. Peri journeyed to Senegal West Africa in the summer of 1998 in search of information about Anna's life before she was brought to Florida. Fluent in Spanish and French, Peri interviewed Griots (local family and community historians) in Senegal, who provided her with important information about the history of Anna's lineage based on her family name—Majigeen Ndiaye. Peri plans to continue her quest for information about her great-grandmother's life in Africa as a personal tribute to her legacy.

KINGSLEY HERITAGE CELEBRATION 2009

On February 21, 2009, a prominent member of the Kingsley family, Dr. Johnnetta Cole, gave the keynote address at the 11th Annual Kingsley Heritage Celebration (Jackson 2009). Much as her cousin Manuel Lebrón did at the 2005 celebration, Dr. Cole, a seventh-generation descendant of Anna and Zephaniah Kingsley, shared her family history and underscored the complex and multiple ways that Zephaniah and Anna Kingsley affected her identity and her understanding of the multiracial and multiethnic families and communities that inform knowledge of the Kingsley site specifically and American history in general (Figure 6.2).

Table 6.3 Anna's family: Descendants of Zephaniah Kingsley, Jr., and Anna Kingsley

1. Zephaniah Kingsley, Jr. (b. 1765 d. 1843) sp: Anna (Anta Majigeen) Ndiaye (b. 1793 d. 1870)
  2. George Kingsley (b. 1807) sp: Anatoile Francoise VaunTravers (m. 1849)
    3. Georgianna Kingsley
    3. Estelle Kingsley
    3. George Kingsley
    3. Zephaniah Kingsley
    3. Anatole Kingsley (*) sp: Jacobo Eleibo
      4. John Kingsley-Eleibo
      4. George Kingsley-Eleibo sp: Mariana Jones
        5. Adolfo Jones Kingsley-Eleibo sp: Martina Medina
          6. Crucito Medina Jones Kingsley-Eleibo
      4. M.? Kingsley-Eleibo
  2. Martha Kingsley Baxter (b. 1809) sp: Cran (? Oran) Baxter
    3. Anna Kingsley Baxter Carroll sp: Charles B. Carroll
    3. Isabella Kingsley Baxter
    3. Julia Catherine Kingsley Baxter
    3. Osmund Edward Kingsley Baxter
    3. Emma Jane Kingsley Baxter Mocs sp: Joseph Mocs
  2. Mary Elizabeth Kingsley (b. 1811) sp: John S. Sammis
    3. Egbert Kingsley-Sammis
    3. George Kingsley-Sammis
    3. Edmund Kingsley-Sammis sp: ? Lizzy
      4. Mary Francis Kingsley-Sammis Lewis (1st wife) sp: A. L. Lewis
        5. James Henry Kingsley-Sammis Lewis sp: Annie Reed Lewis, 2nd wife (Bertha Lewis 1st wife)
          6. James Leonard Kingsley-Sammis Lewis sp: Nelly
          6. Mary Francis Kingsley-Sammis Lewis sp: John T. Betsch
            7. **Johnnetta Kingsley-Sammis Lewis Betsch** sp: Robert Cole (1st husband)
              8. Aaron Cole
              8. Ethan Che Cole
              8. David Cole
            7. **MaVynee Kingsley-Sammis Lewis Betsch**

(Continued)

Table 6.3 (*Continued*)

7. John Kingsley-Sammis Lewis Betsch sp: C. Cresswell, 1st wife
8. Peri Frances Betsch
2. John Maxwell Kingsley (b. 1824)

Source: Duval County Florida Probate Records and Martha E. Davis personal files

Figure 6.2 Kingsley descendant Dr. Johnnetta Cole, NPS Kingsley Heritage Celebration, February 21, 2009, Kingsley Plantation, Jacksonville, Florida (source: NPS/ Paul Haftel)

In 1884, Abraham Lincoln Lewis (1865–1947) married Mary F. Sammis (1865–1923), who was the daughter of Edward Sammis, a Duval County justice of the peace; the granddaughter of Mary Elizabeth Kingsley-Sammis and John S. Sammis; and the great-granddaughter of Zephaniah and Anna Kingsley. Or perhaps a better way to think about the Kingsley-Sammis-Lewis family genealogy is that given by Dr. Cole:

> Well, Anna Kingsley was my maternal great-grandmother, Mary Sammis, Lewis's father's grandmother. Now if you are an anthropologist you could figure that out. Put it another way, Anna Kingsley's grandson,

whose name was Edward G. Sammis, married a woman whose name was Lizzy, who was sometimes called Eliza Willis Sammis. Their eldest daughter, are you with me? . . . You got Anna Kingsley and you got her grandson. What's his name? Edward G. Sammis. He marries . . . Eliza, they have children, their oldest child was Mary Sammis-Lewis. Who was she? She married Abraham Lincoln Lewis, who is my great-grandfather. You just got your Ph.D. in Anthropology!

—Dr. Johnnetta Betsch Cole, keynote address, 11th Annual Kingsley
Heritage Celebration in Jacksonville, Florida, February 21, 2009

Who is Anna Kingsley, and what makes her central to understanding the complexity of the descendant community and its relationship to the Kingsley Plantation? The question of Anna Kingsley and her centrality in discussions of the Kingsley Plantation was posed by Dr. Johnnetta Betsch Cole in her keynote address to the 11th annual Kingsley Heritage Celebration in Jacksonville on February 21, 2009. Dr. Cole is a self-identified African-American woman, a seventh-generation descendant of Anna and Zephaniah Kingsley, a trained anthropologist, and a former President of Spelman College and Bennett College. In the opening remarks of her talk entitled "Sankofa: Looking Back to Go Forward," Cole declared Anna Kingsley her *shero*, a female hero of special note because of her gender and the obstacles of extraordinary size and scope that she had to overcome to achieve her goal. In the case of Anna Kingsley, these obstacles included slavery, racism, sexism, and patriarchy in the 1800s. Standing on the grounds of the Kingsley Plantation, a place she described as difficult for her to visit, Dr. Cole encouraged the enthusiastic and attentive audience to consider making Anna their *shero* as well:

She's a shero for me. Obviously the Park Service thinks so. They invited you here to understand not only about Zephaniah Kingsley but to understand about Anna Kingsley. She is a shero. But I have to ask you, should we remember her as a slave or should we deal with the fact that she was a slave owner? Wasn't she both? Was Anna Kingsley an African or was she an American, or was she both? Were her children, the four sired by Zephaniah Kingsley, were they white or were they black or were they both? Countless lessons I think. All of us are doing our best to learn from being in this extraordinary, this exquisite moment of American history and the history of the world!

—Dr. Johnnetta Betsch Cole, keynote address, 11th Annual Kingsley
Heritage Celebration in Jacksonville, Florida, February 21, 2009

Dr. Cole's provocative descriptive of Anna Kingsley frames the theme and urgency of this discussion. Her narrative helps advance a reinterpretation of notions of citizenship through her presentation and critique of Anna's life, particularly her ability to purchase commodities, including enslaved people for her family's economic benefit. Simultaneously, there were noted limitations with respect to Anna Kingsley's ability to fully exercise her citizenship status, primarily in the area of marriage laws. The state of Florida, for example, prohibited legally sanctioned marriages between blacks and whites until after the passage of the Civil Rights Act in 1964 (Romano 2006; Sollors 1997). Nonetheless, recovering Anna's story through interpretations shared by descendants demonstrates the potency of an analysis that acknowledges the fluidity of roles and relationships in the lives of African people and diasporic communities. Such perspectives are essential in disrupting fixed notions of social place (see Brown 1998, 2000; Gilroy 1991 [1987], 1993a).

KINGSLEY DESCENDANTS AND THE DOMINICAN REPUBLIC CONNECTION

Always talking about the Kingsley story.

—Manuel Lebrón (November 8, 2010, personal communication)

Kingsley-Eliebo

Anthropologist Dr. Martha Ellen Davis and historian Dr. Daniel Schafer (2003) have conducted research on the Kingsley family's Dominican Republic connections. The family migrated to the island when it was under Haitian rule—1822–1844. At that time, Zephaniah Kingsley was pursuing business interest in Haiti and moved members of his family there to live. The information collected by Davis and Schafer help to expand the Kingsley family profile.

Dr. Martha Ellen Davis first became interested in Kingsley family history through Kingsley descendant Crucito Medina Kingsley-Eleibo, whom she met in the late 1970s while pursuing her research interest in folklore and folk traditions in the Dominican Republic. Her collaboration with Crucito Medina Kingsley-Eleibo resulted in the collection of primary and secondary source material on Zephaniah Kingsley's family connections in the Dominican Republic. When I interviewed Dr. Davis regarding her findings, she explained that Crucito is a descendant in the family line of George Kingsley and his wife, Anatoile VaunTravers Kingsley (Table 6.3). George and Anatoile's daughter, Anatole Kingsley, married Jacobo Eleibo, and Crucito is their great-grandson. Members of the Kingsley-Eleibo family still reside in the Puerto Plata area of the Dominican Republic and have lived there since the late 1830s (Martha Davis 2001).

Kingsley-Lebrón

However, it was Lebrón's account of his family's connection to the Kingsley Plantation that brought the story alive for me in ways I had not anticipated. Anna and Zephaniah Kingsley had four children George, John, Mary, and Martha (see Table 6.1). Mary Kingsley Sammis and Martha Kingsley Baxter each married wealthy white men from the New England area and settled in the Jacksonville, Florida, area. George Kingsley and his brother John Maxwell established households in the Dominican Republic, at that time known as Haiti. According to Lebrón's account, his great-great grandmother, Maria, was the great-great-granddaughter of Zephaniah and Anna Kingsley. In other words, Maria's mother was John Maxwell Kingsley's daughter (Sandra Lebrón 1998).

During our conversation in November 2010, Manuel said that when he was growing up he always heard stories about Anna Kingsley. For example, family members said that Anna carried a pouch with gold coins that was always tied to her wrist; she had a house by the beach with attendants; and she always wore long, flowing white gowns. He further recounted that at all family events the Kingsley story is discussed. His family is always talking about the Kingsleys. Manuel indicated that he had first become acquainted with the research being conducted on his family by Dr. Schafer during his visit to the Kingsley Plantation in the mid-1990s as part of his internship (personal communication, November 8, 2010). Schafer has traveled to the Dominican Republic and other places collecting information on the Kingsley family (Schafer 2003), and Manuel Lebrón's family and Dr. Schafer have become friends.

The Kingsley Plantation descendant community provides explicit examples of dynamic and multiple constructions of place in diasporic context. Their interpretations and lived experiences connect the past to the present and expand notions of plantation space.

THE KINGSLEY PLANTATION—A PHYSICAL (AND SOCIAL) REMINDER

The Kingsley Plantation site is located in the state of Florida, east of the city of Jacksonville at the northern tip of Fort George Island, at the Fort George inlet. It was originally home to the Timucua Indians (Milanich 1999 [1996]). Zephaniah Kingsley, Jr., purchased the island in 1817 and owned the plantation until 1839, when he sold it to his nephews Ralph King and Kingsley Beatty Gibbs. Today, the plantation is part of the National Park Service's Timucuan Ecological and Historic Preserve (Figure 6.3). The Preserve was created as part of a 1988 Act—Public Law 100-249—to protect important ecological and cultural resources in northeast Florida (Stowell 1996).

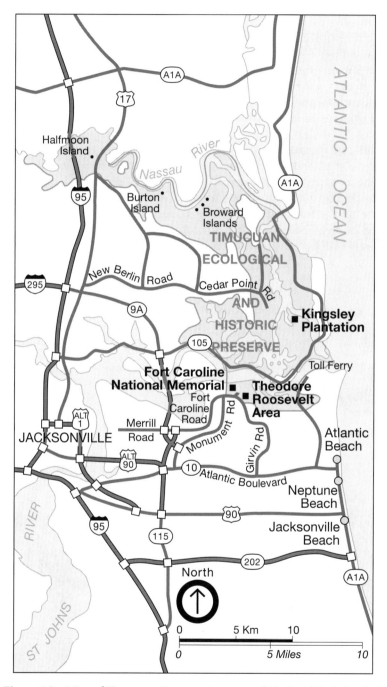

Figure 6.3 Map of Timucuan Preserve (courtesy of National Park Service)

The physical space that forms the Kingsley Plantation site as it existed at the time of Kingsley's ownership includes Zephaniah Kingsley's "big" house (Figure 6.4), Anna Kingsley's "kitchen" house, a barn, and slave cabin remains situated on approximately 720 acres of land with waterway access via the Fort George inlet.

Historian Daniel Stowell (1996) writes that from 1804 until around 1811, planter John Houston McIntosh lived on Fort George Island and planted Sea Island cotton as a commercial enterprise with a labor force of 160–200 enslaved Africans. Zephaniah Kingsley occupied the island between 1812 and 1839. Although his primary business focus was slave trading as opposed to plantation management, Zephaniah Kingsley was considered an important and successful planter. He planted Sea Island cotton and subsistence crops such as sugar cane and rice and maintained orange groves with a labor force of 100–120 enslaved Africans (Stowell 1996).

EXPANDING NOTIONS OF PLACE

Kingsley Plantation is a place that was actively connected—geographically, economically, and socially—to the transatlantic slave trade. Today it remains a physical reminder of slavery in America. The Kingsley

Figure 6.4   Kingsley Plantation House (courtesy of author)

Plantation is enshrined within the political agenda of National Park Service and representations of national heritage in the United States.

The history of the Kingsley Plantation is an interesting and complex combination of people, personalities, and agendas. The Kingsley Plantation on Fort George Island is part of the National Park Service's Timucuan Ecological and Historic Preserve. However, the Kingsley Plantation community extends well beyond the physical boundaries of the Preserve. It includes greater Jacksonville and the surrounding areas from Fernandina (to the north) to St. Augustine (to the south) and all other places where Kingsley descendants and others associated with the plantation live today. Kingsley Plantation and community operate within the context of diaspora space.

Diaspora

An array of diasporas and diaspora studies have entered the anthropological lexicon since the faintly discernable time when "diaspora," which derives from the Greek word *diaspeirein* (to "scatter"), primarily referred to the Jewish diaspora—the uprooting and dispersal of Jewish people. Diaspora theorist Khachig Tölölyan (1996) refers to the transatlantic slave trade period of African diaspora formation as an "exceptional" case, especially when evaluated in relation to the Jewish experience. About the Jewish diaspora experience model and possibilities of other types of diaspora formations he writes:

> This notion [the Jewish model] emphasizes the preservation and/or non-discontinuous evolution of a single, previously available identity, and tends to overlook the possibility that quite loosely related populations possessed of many different, locally circumscribed identities in their homelands, but regarded as "one" in the hostland, can be turned into a diaspora by the gaze of that hostland.
>
> —Tölölyan (1996:13)

Scholars from a variety of disciplines encompassing a range of political perspectives have engaged in theoretical discussions about African diaspora (see Drake 1993; Fikes and Lemon 2002; Hamilton 1990; Harris 1993, 1996; Okpewho et al. 1999; Patterson and Kelly 2000; Scott 1999; Shepperson 1993; Skinner 1993; Thompson 1987; Tölölyan 1996; Uya 1992). Diaspora space expands the context for analyzing plantation realities beyond static and hierarchical characterizations. It allows for examination and incorporation of larger social, historical, and global politics, practices, and processes. For example, the kinship connections and movement as described by Manuel Lebrón—and social realities, challenges, and critiques regarding dealing with issues of race, class, and gender as shared by Dr. Johnnetta Cole—act to broaden ways of thinking about plantations, slavery, and descendants of enslaved Africans. Incorporating descendant voices from a diasporic place perspective gives primacy to the notion of looking back to learn how to move forward as an interpretative lens—a theme underscored by Manuel Lebrón in 2005 and Dr. Cole in 2009 at the Kingsley Heritage Celebration.

CONCLUSION

The Kingsley Plantation and community is a story of the African diaspora. Manuel Lebrón's connection to his great-great-grandparents, whose lives were not geographically restricted solely to the Kingsley Plantation, contributes to a reexamination of the plantation within this wider frame of diaspora space. His recollection of conversations and stories shared within his family about the life and business activities of Zephaniah Kingsley, Jr., born in Bristol, England in 1765, and Anta Majigeen Ndiaye (Anna Kingsley), born in Senegal, West Africa in 1793, underscores the importance of looking at Kingsley Plantation as both a product of the African diaspora and a place where affected people can examine meanings and associations in the present. Manuel Lebrón emphasized the fact that the Kingsley story is an important part of the family life and lore for his family. This is an alternative to singularly focused notions of plantations as bounded, which the National Park Service emphasizes when focusing, during the annual Kingsley Heritage Celebration, on the traditional roles of the people who lived on the plantation. Lebrón's perspective stimulates a more dynamic view of the plantation.

Analyzing plantation spaces as diasporic sites has theoretical underpinning in the work of Matory (2005), Scott (1999), and Clarke and Thomas (2006). Matory examines the formation of community from a diasporic space perspective expressed through daily acts of ritual and exchange that are constantly being negotiated. Scott (1999) calls for maintaining an ongoing debate about denaturalizing signifiers of slavery as a strategic imperative that must be continually renewed through the creation of new traditions of critical discourse about the transatlantic slave trade and the dispersion of African people.[1] And Clarke and Thomas (2006) focus on global dynamics such as transatlantic slavery and their current effects by looking at the active role individuals play in contextualizing their own experiences. The story of the Kingsley Plantation challenges stereotypical characterizations of plantation life and evokes other ways of thinking about plantations and their meanings in the future.

In their detailed analysis of 122 former plantations, now tourist sites in the U.S. South, Jennifer Eichstedt and Stephen Small, in their book *Representations of Slavery* (2002), note:

> Prominent plantation heritage sites tell a particular type of story (white- and elite-centric) to a particular kind of tourist (white). These stories emphasize the hard work, civility, and ingenuity of plantation owners (who are almost invariably male) and provide a largely reverential characterization of gendered kinship relations in southern society, though there are variations across states.
>
> —Eichstedt and Small (2002:6)

Soliciting and incorporating the narratives of Anna Kingsley's descendants expand this narrow view of plantation life. The Kingsley Plantation community compels an interrogation of more complex notions of family and community in the context of the transatlantic slave trade. The multinational and multiracial Kingsley family associations challenge bounded representations of plantations in terms of geography, race/ethnicity, and black/white dichotomies of slavery in the U.S. South.

Chapter 7

CONCLUSION

While anthropological descriptions of place have remained relatively monological, places themselves are fertilized into being through a confluence of voices. Places are complex constructions of social histories, personal and interpersonal experiences, and selective memory.

—Miriam Kahn (1996:167)

The representation of plantations as dynamic and diasporic spaces is an underrepresented perspective in the interpretive context of national heritage in the United States. Specifically, there are gaps in the interpretive sphere that limit how plantations are seen, understood, and experienced today by visitors to former antebellum plantation sites. These gaps exist because the production of knowledge about plantations has primarily been articulated from a plantation owner perspective—typically that of the white male elite. This perspective is branded, marketed, and projected to the general public as a product and an asset of historical significance without critique. In the case of the Charles Pinckney National Historic Site in South Carolina, for example, the United States Department of the Interior originally established the site to interpret and represent the life of Charles Pinckney. The Department of the Interior later expanded the original mandate to include the interpretation of the lives of all the site's inhabitants—enslaved and free (Blythe 2000). The earlier, singular representation of Pinckney ignored enslaved Africans and their descendants, thereby fixing them in static categories. The National Park Service's corrective, however, although it resulted in the inclusion of enslaved Africans, still requires an intervention that counters simplistic representations in the interpretive process. Through the strategic and conscious use of descendant voices as a primary asset, my analysis constructs a rubric of knowledge that informs interpretation of plantation sites in more nuanced and critical ways. The incorporation of descendant voices from an African diasporic place perspective is a corrective to interpretations that limit the social, temporal, and geographic lens through which plantations can be seen contemporarily.

To go beyond the ubiquitous representation of former antebellum plantation sites in the United States as synonymous with *Gone with the Wind*, we need to address several key issues. These include (1) critiquing issues of categorization that posit plantations, plantation communities, and enslaved laborers as static (fixed in time) and monolithic; (2) interrogating processes that subjugate knowledge and limit holistic representations and interpretations of the life and labor of enslaved Africans and their descendants (that is, critiquing interpretations of enslaved Africans as powerless and without agency, particularly in terms of affecting their future and that of their descendants); and (3) conducting active and ongoing interpretations of antebellum and postbellum plantations as dynamic sites of history and heritage, particularly in terms of labor roles and responsibilities and family and community relationships and associations that span local and global boundaries.

David Valentine's perspective is useful in contextualizing problems of categorization and representation raised in this discussion. He argues that the meanings that categories have in the world are never neutral (Valentine 2007). It is important to ask questions and interrogate meanings. Recognition and acknowledgment of descendant knowledge and descendant narratives in the interpretation and preservation process as a cultural heritage resource are critical interventions. Subjugated knowledge can be embodied within individuals as well as communities that have typically been ignored or disproportionately represented as peripheral (Collins 1991; Foucault 1980 [1972]).

This book has addressed several key questions: (1) In which ways does knowledge shared by enslaved Africans and their descendants living in, or associated with, plantation spaces through stories, rituals, traditions, and memories help inform interpretation of U.S. plantation sites in the contemporary present? (2) What tools, questions, and methods can be used to research and profile people and communities whose stories have gone untold or have been relegated to the margins of mainstream public discourse of American history? More specifically, how do the ways in which African and African-American history and heritage are represented (or not) at National Heritage sites and other public sites deemed to be of historical significance inform our knowledge of U.S. history and culture? (3) What role can heritage and heritage resource management practices play in expanding public understanding of antebellum and postbellum plantations as communities and sites of knowledge through incorporation of descendant voices?

America's history and heritage are intertwined with the transatlantic slave trade, plantation agriculture, and the history and heritage of enslaved Africans and their descendants, who developed strategies for living and strategies for surviving in antebellum and postbellum plantation environs. This legacy is neither the beginning nor the end of the story; rather, it is part of the fabric of U.S. American culture. It is a story that continues to be reinterpreted with each new generation.

This book underscores the significance of analyzing the legacy—from the founding fathers to former President George W. Bush, to President Barack Obama and First Lady Michelle Obama—of the transatlantic slave trade, antebellum and postbellum plantation spaces, through the incorporation of descendant voices. For example, when President Bush signed the National Heritage Areas Act of 2006, it authorized the establishment of the Gullah/Geechee Cultural Heritage Corridor. This historic legislation, championed by Rep. James E. Clyburn (D) of South Carolina, opened the door for new interpretations of American history. However, the idea of the African experience in antebellum plantation communities as a quintessentially American story is all the more relevant to the general public because of Michelle Obama's connection to Friendfield Plantation, a former antebellum rice plantation. Her ancestral journey from slavery to the White House and her desire to understand, as well as frame her family's journey in the context of other such journeys embedded in the fabric of America's story, contemporarily and historically, is representative of the theme and aim of this book.

Descendants consulted in this book shed light on broader dynamics of family, community, and the impact of global and historical processes on everyday experiences. But their stories and observations have often been misrepresented or underrepresented at public heritage sites, in media representations, and by scholars. To counteract this situation, the rubric of "knowledge" (see also Boellstroff 2009) can be used as a framework for incorporating descendant voices, which have often been subjugated, as another way of understanding plantation spaces. In other words, descendant voices, narratives, and stories contribute to the formulation of a rubric of knowledge that sidesteps fixed categorizations and challenges and expands generic interpretations (Jackson 2011).

Examples of underrepresentation of accounts are those told by Mrs. Obama, Ms. Gaillard, and Mr. Lebrón. Mrs. Obama's story underscores the irony of the past by illuminating challenges faced in confronting a contested past. In Mrs. Obama's case, it is an ancestral past that includes systematic exploitation under the U.S. American system of chattel slavery and a family's journey from slavery through segregation to freedom. At the same time, it is a story of the power of the past—overcoming and learning from the past. This journey is because it is this same journey, from slavery to freedom, that placed Mrs. Obama in the role of First Lady of the United States of America.

In the case of Ms. Gaillard, there is also an underrepresentation of the meaning of home, exemplified by her reaction to seeing the torn-off roof of her former slave cabin home. Her connection to the plantation, which to her was home, offers an interpretation of a place ("the" plantation) many would rather forget that complicates fixed representations of postbellum plantation life.

And finally, Mr. Lebrón's account of his association with the Kingsley Plantation and participation in the annual Kingsley Heritage Celebration provides an expanded representation of place that goes beyond the interpretive boundaries delineated by the National Park Service's Timucuan Ecological and Historic Preserve. It incorporates the concept of diaspora space as a critical analytical frame. In Mr. Lebrón's critique we see how descendant knowledge, understood from a diaspora space perspective, enables the reimagination of plantations to include an interrogation of meaning in the contemporary moment—beyond temporally and geographically bounded notions of place.

Knowledge production, particularly the problem of privileging certain knowledge, is an active act of engagement (Jackson 2011). Descendants such as Mrs. Obama, Ms. Gaillard, Mr. Lebrón, and the many unnamed Africans on plantations like Jehossee inform deeper, more complex meanings of and connections to plantations, and they challenge static characterizations. Without the lessons shared by people such as Ms. Mattie Gaillard and others in the community of Mount Pleasant and elsewhere, my own writings and interpretations of plantations would have been in danger of reproducing the same limiting portrayals and marginal placement of enslaved Africans, their descendants, and postbellum plantation communities. Instead their stories re-analyze plantations and antebellum and postbellum plantation communities and advance different readings of life in these spaces today.

Reconfiguring how we talk about Africans (enslaved and free) and their descendants in plantation spaces contributes to dismantling entrenched systems of representation that continue to conflate the conditions of slavery that Africans suffered with an essentialized nature of "being a slave." By disassociating slavery-as-a-condition—produced through a specific sequence of social-political-legal-economic processes—from the label or category "slave," we discursively "free" all descendants of Africans in America from a form of cultural enslavement in which blackness comes to be perpetually linked to meanings and associations consistent with the label "slave." The choice of words is the difference between existing in a perpetual state of discursive (re)enslavement of being forced to embody the full weight of the chain of marginality, or expanding how we think about, research, and theorize a growing range of possibilities for representing the diversity of cultural experiences associated with postbellum plantation spaces as designated public heritage areas of national import.

Dialogue about slavery, which is moored to ideological, social, and physical remnants of plantations, is ongoing. Knowledge created through stories, observations, lived experiences, and critiques offered by the people affected by our work as scholars and heritage professionals, for example, is an active act of participation in shaping public memory. In this discussion, I have linked an ethnographic research approach to the construction of memory, informing how we understand and experience the legacy of slavery and the transatlantic slave trade in the United States.

The experience of slavery must be attended to in the context of Europe's global expansion. However, even in the act of revisiting and representing history there remains the problem of fixing people in that history. In his critique of the ethnographic approach, Caribbean and African diaspora-focused scholar Edouard Glissant (1989) offers a warning and a reminder to anthropologists to remain critical in the application of their research tools and approach. Although the ethnographic method creates a detailed snapshot in time of the people being represented, it cannot be thought of as the definitive means of portraying the totality of their lived experiences, regardless of intent. In other words, the solicitation of descendant knowledge within specific families and communities should be an ongoing process (Jackson 2011). Through such solicitation, memories of descendants of the enslaved, constructed in the contemporary present, constitute additional sources of knowledge that can contribute to continually rethinking plantation spaces.

The experience of slavery in America is not so distant that we cannot develop more nuanced interpretations of people's lives. Other scholars have argued for more dynamic and holistic approaches to representations and have called for transnational approaches that recognize the African diaspora as a critical tool and site of analysis for understanding and critiquing the impact of global processes of change (Apter 1991; Brown 2005; Clarke and Thomas 2006; Fabian 2007; Gilroy 1993b; Lovejoy 2000; Matory 2005; Scott 1999). Building on the work of their scholarship and incorporating descendant knowledge about plantation experiences obtained through ethnographic, ethnohistorical, and oral-history research, this book illuminates the agency of enslaved

Africans. For example, a vast majority of former rice, cotton, and indigo plantations located along the southeast coast of the United States from North Carolina to Florida were majority African (Wood 1974). This was not only because of the sheer demand for enslaved African labor but also because of the need for technological knowledge and expertise in such areas as rice cultivation, which many enslaved Africans brought with them to this region during the period of the transatlantic slave trade. Today, many of these former antebellum plantations are considered of national and international importance. Others are located within federally designated National Heritage Areas—recognized as containing material, cultural, ecological, and historical resources to be preserved and interpreted for future generations.

POSTSCRIPT: ANOTHER EXAMPLE OF RECASTING THE EXPERIENCE OF
ENSLAVED AFRICANS

The Great Dismal Swamp project is a recent example of a public heritage initiative to advance new ways of understanding the experience of enslaved Africans in U.S. history (Breen 2011). Research being conducted in the Great Dismal Swamp by historical archaeologist, Dan Sayers, in partnership with the National Park Service, the U.S. Fish and Wildlife Service and Nature Preserve, and the North Carolina Division of State Historic Sites and Properties, highlights ways in which institutional legitimacy at a national level can help address gaps in the interpretive record of the experiences of enslaved Africans. The Great Dismal Swamp is an 112,000 acre public nature preserve that straddles the line between North Carolina and Virginia. It is currently owned by the U.S. Fish and Wildlife Service and was once home to communities of people, primarily enslaved Africans, escaping slavery. Enslaved Africans and their descendants used the Dismal Swamp as home and haven from chattel slavery, establishing entire communities that remained active from the 1600s through the early nineteenth century, according to the material record being compiled by Sayers (2007).

Critical examination of the Great Dismal Swamp as a public site of national significance illustrates the three issues I raise concerning how to effectively expand singularly focused representations of former antebellum plantations and advance a wider view. By systematically evaluating how each issue is addressed in the case of the Dismal Swamp, my work and this analysis highlights ways in which institutional legitimacy can more holistically counter gaps in the public representation of marginalized groups in U.S. American history. Sites such as the Dismal Swamp disrupt interpretations of geographically bounded notions of plantation spaces to incorporate a diasporic or dynamic reading of the experiences of enslaved Africans and their descendants. Specifically, the timeliness of the proposed prescriptive by the National Park Service of establishing a permanent exhibition to provide more detail about lives of those who sought to escape slavery (Breen 2011) highlights ways of challenging the problem of categorizing enslaved laborers in monolithic terms—as simply enslaved. First of all, the Dismal Swamp project reveals how enslaved people pursued other tactics to circumvent their condition of enslavement by leaving their environs. Second, it reveals how uncovering knowledge can showcase the agency and ingenuity of enslaved Africans who created communities outside antebellum plantations. Third, it offers an interpretation that counters the view of plantations as static sites of history and heritage. This project also reveals the movement of enslaved African people from plantations to freedom that included destinations other than in the North.

However, the story (and the proposed story for the permanent exhibit) of the Dismal Swamp can be broadened—linking the past to the present in instructive ways that challenge simplistic representations. For example, a gernerally implied dichotomy depicts enslaved Africans as either passive people living on the plantation or escapees who resisted plantation life. Consequently, the continuum of strategies for living and surviving that enslaved Africans employed is underrepresented. I have described the need for constructing a rubric of knowledge to incorporate descendant voices as a key cultural resource; and ethnographic and ethnohistorical methodology as a cultural anthropological intervention that advance ways of connecting the past to the present. Use of archival records can lead to the construction of kinship associations that could be used to locate descendants. Through application of this methodology the presence of extended communities (Jackson 2004, 2006), might help to identify sophisticated and dynamic systems of communication (see Turner 1949) between plantation and Dismal Swamp residents. Interviewing descendants might reveal that there were symbols or directions showing/teaching people how to enter and exit the Swamp. Finally, oral histories with descendants could contribute to identifying patterns of diasporic connections—they might show that multiethnic and multiracial kinship associations were developed possibly spanning local and global boundaries (Jackson 2009, 2011).

NOTES

CHAPTER 1

1. The archaeological research of the late Charles Fairbanks of the University of Florida is notable (1974). His excavations of Kingsley Plantation slave cabins in northeast Florida, initiated in 1968, led the way for future archaeological studies of the lives of enslaved African people and their descendants in antebellum plantation spaces (Davidson 2008).

2. Plantations chosen for this research study (Boone Hall in Mount Pleasant, Snee Farm in Mount Pleasant, South Carolina and Kingsley Plantation in Jacksonville, Florida) were part of National Park Service (NPS) funded research projects to study African life in antebellum and postbellum plantation spaces (see Gibbs 2006; Jackson 2006).

3. Others scholars, such as de Certeau and Rendell (1984) and Pred and Watts (1992), give primacy to everyday acts of living or the pursuit of meaning articulated through traditions, customs, and ritual on local and specific levels, as a means of understanding and explaining transformation.

CHAPTER 3

1. Alex Haley was the author of *Roots*, published in 1976. The book spent forty-six weeks on the New York Times Best Seller List. It provoked a cultural sensation in America and around the world, especially with the release of the made for television series, *Roots*, which was based on the book. Haley made people talk about the slave roots of an African-American family.

2. Excerpt from detailed sale information posted on December 26, 2009, at www.millikenforestry.com.

Friendfield Plantation

Type	Real estate
Acres	3,264.6
Total price	
Price/Acre	0
Status	New listing—active
State	SC
County	Georgetown

Friendfield, which began as a rice plantation and has been developed into a high-quality duck and quail hunting property, is now for sale. The existing plantation house was constructed in 1930, following the plans of the original house, which burned in 1926. The house overlooks ancient moss-draped live oaks and abundant rice fields now used for duck hunting. Friendfield consists of 3,100 acres with more than 2,000 + acres of managed quail woods, 250 acres of controlled and managed rice fields, 75 acres of pastures, and deep-water access to the Sampit River. Friendfield has all amenities necessary for an impressive hunting and recreational property. See http://millikenforestry.com/Services/RealEstateListings/tabid/79/agentType/View/PropertyID/34/Default.aspx, accessed October 19, 2010.

Chapter 4

1. Public access to Jehossee is currently restricted pending completion and implementation of a more comprehensive heritage resource management plan by the U.S. Fish and Wildlife Service, according refuge management.

Chapter 6

1. As a proponent of African diasporic criticism, Scott (1999), along with others (Apter 1991; Brown 1998, 2000; Clarke and Thomas 2006; Gilroy 1993a; Hall 1996) has advocated analyses that critique the intellectual processes that subjugate knowledge about African people. Their approaches in recognizing the dynamism of African diasporic cultural forms can be contrasted against limiting constructions. The scholarship of sociologist E. Franklin Frazier (1942, 1957 [1949]), for example, in equating "slavery" with blackness and "Africa" as culturally void, stands in direct contrast to African diaspora criticism in the construction and representation of Africa and Africans in the Americas. Scott describes the process of interrogating meanings and objectives behind intellectual inquiry and research pursuits concerning black diaspora communities as invoking "tradition." He defines tradition as an active process (Scott 1999:115).

References

Adams, Paul C., Steven Hoelscher, and Karen E. Till, eds. (2001) *Textures of Place: Exploring Humanist Geographies*. Minneapolis: University of Minnesota Press.

Alberts, Sheldon (2009) From slavery to the White House: Michelle Obama First lady's roots are traced to mixed-race family. *The Gazette* (Montreal), October 9, 2009.

Allston, Robert, F. W. (1843) *Memoir of the Introduction and Planting of Rice in South Carolina: A Description of the Grass*. Charleston, SC: Miller and Browne.

Alston, Lee J., and Kyle D. Kaufmann (1998) Up, down, and off the agricultural ladder: New evidence and implications of agricultural mobility for blacks in the Postbellum South. *Agricultural History* 72(2):263–79.

Amselle, Jean-Loup (1998[1990]) *Mestizo Logics: Anthropology of Identity in Africa and Elsewhere*. Claudia Royal, trans. Stanford, CA: Stanford University Press.

Anderson, Benedict (1991) *Imagined Communities: Reflections on the Origin and Spread of Nationalism*. New York: Verso.

Antonowicz, Anton (2009) Michelle Obama: Trace her amazing journey from Slave Street to the White House. *The Daily Mirror* (Mirror.co.uk News), January 19, 2009, 3 Star Edition.

Apter, Andrew (1991) Herskovits's heritage: Rethinking syncretism in the African diaspora. *Diaspora: A Journal of Transnational Studies* 1(3):235–60.

——— (2002) On African origins: Creolization and connaissance in Haitian vodou. *American Ethnologist* 29(2):233–60.

Aptheker, James E. (1951) *A Documentary History of the Negro People in the United States: From the Reconstruction Era to 1910*. New York: The Citadel Press.

Bagwell, James E. (2000) *Rice Gold: James Hamilton Couper and Plantation Life on the Georgia Coast*. Macon, GA: Mercer University Press.

Bailey, Cornelia Walker (2000) *God, Dr. Buzzard, and the Bolito Man*. New York: Anchor Books.

Baker, Lee D. (1998) *From Savage to Negro: Anthropology and the Construction of Race, 1896–1954*. Berkeley and Los Angeles: University of California Press.

Ball, Charles (1859) *Fifty Years in Chains (The Life of an American Slave)*. New York: B. Dayton.

Ball, Edward (1998) *Slaves in the Family*. New York: Ballantine Books.

Bancroft, Frederick (1959 [1931]) *Slave Trading in the Old South*. New York: Frederick Ungar Publishing Co.

Barber, John W. (1969 [1840]) *History of the Amistad Captives*. New York: Arno Press.

Bargar, B. D. (1970) *Royal South Carolina 1719–1763*. Columbia: University of South Carolina.

Bascom, William R. (1976) Acculturation among the Gullah Negroes. In *Shaping Southern Society*. T. H. Breen, ed., pp. 59–66. New York: Oxford University Press.

Bee, Robert L. (1974) *Patterns and Processes: An Introduction to Anthropological Strategies for the Study of Sociocultural Change*. New York: The Free Press.

Behre, Robert (1997) New challenges for plantation—Investor works on keeping Friendfield together. *The Post and Courier* (Charleston, SC), July 27, 1997.

Berlin, Ira (1998) *Many Thousands Gone: The First Two Centuries of Slavery in North America*. Cambridge, MA: Harvard University Press.

Berlin, Ira, and Philip D. Morgan, eds. (1991) *The Slaves' Economy: Independent Production by Slaves in the Americas*. London: Frank Cass & Co.

––––––– (1993) *Cultivation and Culture: Labor and the Shaping of Slave Life in the Americas*. Charlottesville and London: University Press of Virginia.

Betsch, Peri Frances (2001) Interview, Atlanta, Georgia, October 2.

Betts, Edwin M. (1944) *Thomas Jefferson's Garden Book, 1766–1824*. Philadelphia: The American Philosophical Society.

Bhabha, Homi K. (1990) Third Space. In *Identity, Community, Culture, Difference*. J. Rutherford, ed., pp. 201–07. London: Lawrence and Wishart.

––––––– (1994) *The Location of Culture*, reprinted 2002. New York: Routledge.

Blassingame, John W. (1979[1972]) *The Slave Community: Plantation Life in the Antebellum South*. New York: Oxford University Press.

Blythe, R. (2000) *Charles Pinckney National Historic Site Historic Resource Study*. Atlanta: National Park Service, U.S. Department of the Interior.

Boas, Franz (1974 [1904]) The history of anthropology. In *The Shaping of American Anthropology: 1883–1911, A Franz Boas Reader*, George W. Stocking Jr., ed., pp. 23–36. New York: Basic Books.

––––––– (1996 [1920]) The methods of ethnology. In *Anthropological Theory: An Introductory History*, R. Jon McGee and Richard L. Warms, eds., pp. 130–37. Mountain View, CA: Mayfield Publishing Company.

Boellstorff, Tom (2005) *The Gay Archipelago: Sexuality and Nation in Indonesia*. Princeton, NJ: Princeton University Press.

––––––– (2009) Nuri's testimony: HIV/AIDS in Indonesia and bare knowledge. *American Ethnologist* 36(2):351–63.

Booth, Sally S. (1971) *Hung, Strung, & Potted: A History of Eating in Colonial America*. New York: Clarkson N. Potter.

Breen, T. H., ed. (1976) *Shaping Southern Society: The Colonial Experience*. New York: Oxford University Press.

Breen, Tom (2011) *In the Great Dismal Swamp*. Associated Press (AP), July 4, 2011.

Brooks, George E. (1993) *Landlords and Strangers: Ecology, Society, and Trade in Western Africa, 1000–1630*. Boulder, CO: Westview Press.

Brown, Ellen P., ed. (1992) Successful small-scale irrigation in the Sahel. *World Bank Technical Paper Number 171*. Washington, D.C.: International Bank for Reconstruction and Development.

Brown, Henry ("H") (2000) Interview, Mount Pleasant, South Carolina, June 23.

Brown, Jacqueline Nassy (1998) Black Liverpool, Black-America, and the gendering of diasporic space. *Cultural Anthropology* 13(3):291–325.

———— (2000) Enslaving history: Narratives on local whiteness in a black Atlantic port. *American Anthropological Association* 27(2):340–70.

———— (2005) *Dropping Anchor, Setting Sail: Geographies of Race in Black Liverpool.* Princeton, NJ: Princeton University Press.

Brown, Peter (2000) Interview, Mount Pleasant, South Carolina, 1 July.

Brownell, Blaine A., and David R. Goldfield, eds. (1977) *The City in Southern History: The Growth of Urban Civilization in the South.* Port Washington, N.Y.: Kennikat Press.

Buchli, V., and G. Lucas, eds. (2001) *Archaeologies of the Contemporary Past.* London: Routledge.

Buddenhagen, I. W., and G. J. Persley, eds. (1978) *Rice in Africa.* New York: Academic Press.

Burns, Allan (1993) *Maya in Exile, Guatamalans in Florida.* Philadelphia: Temple University Press.

Burton, Vernon (1985) *In My Father's House Are Many Mansions.* Chapel Hill: University of North Carolina Press.

Butler, Judith (1993) *Bodies That Matter.* New York: Routledge.

Campbell, John (1991) As "a kind of freeman"?: Slaves' market-related activities in the South Carolina upcountry, 1800–1860. In *The Slaves' Economy: Independent Production by Slaves in the Americas*, Ira Berlin and Philip D. Morgan, eds., pp.131–69. London: Frank Cass & Co.

Campbell, Mavis C. (1993) *Back to Africa: George Ross & the Maroons: From Nova Scotia to Sierra Leone.* Trenton, NJ: Africa World Press.

Carney, Judith A. (1993) From hands to tutors: African expertise in the South Carolina rice economy. *Agricultural History* 67(3):1–30.

———— (2001) *Black Rice: The African Origins of Rice Cultivation in the Americas.* Cambridge, MA: Harvard University Press.

Carter, Allison (2008) Tourism and national heritage. In *Encyclopedia of Race and Racism*, John Hartwell Moore, ed., Volume 3, pp. 134–43. Detroit, MI: MacMillan Reference USA.

Chafe, William H., Raymond Gavins, and Robert Korstad, eds. (2001) *Remembering Jim Crow.* New York: The New Press.

Chakrabarty, Dipesh (2000) *Provincializing Europe: Postcolonial Thought and Historical Difference.* Princeton, NJ: Princeton University Press.

Chambers, Erve (2006) *Heritage Matters: Heritage, Culture, History, and Chesapeake Bay.* College Park, MD: A Maryland Sea Grant Publication.

———— (2010 [2000]) *Native Tours—The Anthropology of Travel and Tourism.* Long Grove, IL: Waveland Press.

Charles, Tommy (1986) *An Archaeological Reconnaissance Survey of Jehossee Island (38CH848).* Columbia: South Carolina Institute of Archaeology and Anthropology, University of South Carolina.

Charleston Area Convention and Tourist Bureau website (n.d.) Charleston Museum 2008 program exhibit, "From Slave to Sharecropper," www.drivetocharleston.com/visitors/events_news/charleston-news/exhibit_to_highlight_african_american_experiences_in_the_lowcountry_after_the_civil_war-906, accessed January 5, 2011.

Charleston Private Equity LLC website (n.d.) www.charleston-southcarolina.us/Attractions/BooneHallPlantation.html, accessed January 5, 2011.

Chibbaro, Anthony (1999) *Images of America: South Carolina's Lowcountry.* Charleston: Arcadia Publishing.

Childs, Arney R., ed. (1953) *Rice Planter and Sportsman: The Recollections of J. Motte Alston, 1821–1909.* Columbia: University of South Carolina Press.

Clark, Andrew F. (1999) *From Frontier to Backwater: Economy and Society in the Upper Senegal Valley West Africa 1850–1920.* Lanham, MD: University Press of America.

Clarke, John Henry, ed. (1996) *Critical Lessons in Slavery and the Slavetrade: Essential Studies and Commentaries on Slavery, in General, and the African Slavetrade, in Particular.* Richmond, VA: Native Son Publishers.

Clarke, Kamari, and Deborah Thomas (2006) *Globalization and Race: Transformations in the Cultural Production of Blackness.* Durham, NC: Duke University Press.

Cleere, H. F., ed. (1989) *Archaeological Heritage Management in the Modern World.* Boston: Unwin Hyman.

Clifford, James (1997) *Routes.* Cambridge, MA: Harvard University Press.

Clifton, J. M. (1985) Jehossee Island: The antebellum South's largest rice plantation. *Agricultural History* 59:56–65.

Clinton, Catherine, and Nina Sibler, eds. (1992) *Divided Houses: Gender and Civil War.* New York: Oxford University.

Coakley, Elizabeth (2000) Interview, Mount Pleasant, South Carolina, June 26.

Cole, Johnnetta B., ed. (1988) *Anthropology for the Nineties.* New York: The Free Press.

——— (2001) Interview, Atlanta, Georgia, October 3.

Collins, Patricia Hill (1991) *Black Feminist Thought: Knowledge, Consciousness, and the Politics of Empowerment.* New York: Routledge.

Commager, Henry S. (1960) *The Era of Reform, 1830–1860.* Princeton: Van Nostrand.

Conklin, Harold C. (1957) *Hanunoo Agriculture: A Report on an Integral System of Shifting Cultivation in the Philippines.* Rome: Food and Agriculture Organization (FAO) of the United Nations.

Connah, Graham (1987) *African Civilizations: Precolonial Cities and States in Tropical Africa: An Archaeological Perspective.* New York: Cambridge University Press.

Conneau, Theophilus (1976) *A Slaver's Log Book or 20 Years' Residence in Africa.* Englewood Cliffs, NJ: Prentice Hall.

Connerton, Paul (1989) *How Societies Remember.* Cambridge: Cambridge University Press.

Cooper, Frederick, Thomas C. Holt, and Rebecca J. Scott (2000) *Beyond Slavery: Explorations of Race, Labor, and Citizenship in Postemancipation Societies.* Chapel Hill: University of North Carolina Press.

Corse, Carlita Doggett (1931) *The Key to the Golden Islands.* Chapel Hill: University of North Carolina Press.

Creel, Margaret W. (1988) *"A Peculiar People": Slave Religion and Community-Culture among the Gullahs.* New York: New York University Press.

Cross, Wilbur (2008) *Gullah Culture in America.* Westport, CT: Praeger Publishers.

Crouch, David, ed. (1999) *Leisure/Tourism Geographies: Practices and Geographical Knowledge.* New York: Routledge.

Cuguano, Quobna O. (1999 [1787]) *Thoughts and Sentiments on the Evil and Wicked Traffic of the Slavery and Commerce of the Human Species.* New York: Penguin Books.

Curtin, Philip D., ed. (1967) *African Remembered: Narratives by West Africans from the Era of the Slave Trade*. Madison: University of Wisconsin Press.

—— (1998) *The Rise and Fall of the Plantation Complex*. Cambridge: Cambridge University Press.

Cusick, Heidi H. (1995) *Soul and Spice: African Cooking in the Americas*. San Francisco: Chronicle Books.

Daise, Ronald (1986) *Reminiscences of Sea Island Heritage*. Orangeburg, SC: Sandlapper Publishing.

—— (2010) *Traveling Highway 17 in Search of the Soul of the Gullah*. Heritage Matters, NPS, U.S. Department of the Interior, Fall 2010, p. 4.

Davidson, James M. (2008) *Interim Report of Investigations of the University of Florida Historical Archaeological Field School: Kingsley Plantation (8Du108), Timucuan Ecological and Historic Preserve, National Park Service, Duval County, Florida*. Submitted to the National Park Service, Southeast Archaeological Center, Tallahassee, Florida.

Davis, Allison, and Burleigh B. Gardner (1941) *Deep South: A Social Anthropological Study of Caste and Class*. Chicago: University of Chicago Press.

Davis, Angela (1983 [1981]) *Women, Race, & Class*. New York: Vintage Books.

Davis, Edwin A., and William Ransom Hogan (1954) *The Barber of Natchez*. Baton Rouge: Louisiana State University Press.

Davis, Martha (2001) Interview, Gainesville, Florida, June 30.

de Certeau, Michel, and Steven Rendall (trans.) (1984) *The Practice of Everyday Life*. Berkeley and Los Angeles: University of California Press.

DeDatta, Surajit K. (1981) *Principles and Practices of Rice Production*. New York: John Wiley & Sons.

Deetz, James (1996) *In Small Things Forgotten: An Archaeology of Early American Life*. New York: Anchor Books.

Delany, Martin (1970 [1861–1862]) *Blake or the Huts of America*. Boston: Beacon Press.

Derby, Doris A. (1980) *Black Women Basket Makers: A Study of Domestic Economy in Charleston County, South Carolina*, dissertation, anthropology, Urbana-Champaign, University of Illinois.

Dethloff, Henry C. (1988) *A History of the American Rice Industry, 1685–1985*. College Station: Texas A&M University Press.

Dixon, Ethel (1987) *Big Mama's Old Black Pot Recipes*. Alexandria, LA: Stoke Gabriel Press.

Doar, David (1970 [1936]) *Rice and Rice Planting in the South Carolina Low Country*. Charleston: The Charleston Museum.

Dollard, John (1957) *Caste and Class in a Southern Town*. Garden City, NJ: Doubleday Anchor Books.

Dorr, David F. (1999) *A Colored Man Round the World*. Ann Arbor: University of Michigan Press.

Drake, St. Clair (1990) *Black Folk Here and There: An Essay in History and Anthropology*. Los Angeles: University of California Center for Afro-American Studies.

—— (1993) Diaspora studies and pan-Africanism. In *Global Dimensions of the African Diaspora* (2nd ed.), J. E. Harris, ed., pp. 451–514. Washington, D.C.: Howard University Press.

Drayton, John (1972 [1802]) *A View of South Carolina*. Columbia: University of South Carolina Press.

Du Bois, W. E. B. (1961 [1903]) *The Souls of Black Folk*. Greenwich, CT: Fawcett Publications.

Dunn, Richard S. (1972) *Sugar and Slaves: The Rise of the Planter Class in the English West Indies, 1624–1713*. New York: W. W. Norton & Company.

——— (1976) The English Sugar Islands and the founding of South Carolina. In *Shaping Southern Society*, T. H. Breen, ed., pp. 48–58. New York: Oxford University Press.

Dusinberre, William (1996) *Them Dark Days: Slavery in the American Rice Swamps*. New York: Oxford University Press.

East Florida Papers Gainesville, FL: University of Florida PKY Library of Florida History, microfilm file 55A, reel 97.

Easterby, J. H. (1928) William Aiken. In *Dictionary of American Biography*, Vol.1., Allen Johnson, ed., pp. 128–29. New York: Charles Scribner's Sons.

——— ed. (1945) *The South Carolina Rice Plantation as Revealed in the Papers of Robert F. Allston*. Chicago: University of Chicago Press.

Edgar, W. B. (1991) *Historic Snee Farm: A Documentary Record*. Columbia: University of South Carolina Department of History.

Eichstedt, Jennifer L., and Stephen Small (2002) *Representations of Slavery: Race and Ideology in Southern Plantation Museums*. Washington, D.C.: Smithsonian Institution Press.

Ellis, Jesse, Sr. (2000) Interview, Mount Pleasant, South Carolina, June 13.

Eltis, David (2000) *The Rise of African Slavery in the Americas*. Cambridge: Cambridge University Press.

Eltis, David, Stephen D. Behrendt, David Richardson, and Herbert S. Klein, eds. (1999) *The Trans-Atlantic Slave Trade: A Database on CD-ROM*. Record id = 13933. Cambridge: Cambridge University Press.

Eltis, David, Frank D. Lewis, and Kenneth L. Sokoloff, eds. (2004) *Slavery and the Development of the Americas*. Cambridge: Cambridge University Press.

Epperson, Terrence W. (1999) Constructing difference: The social and spatial order of the Chesapeake Plantation. In *"I, too, am America": Archaeological Studies of African-American Life*, Theresa A. Singleton, ed., pp. 159–72. Charlottesville: University Press of Virginia.

Equiano, Olaudah (1969 [1837]) *The Life of Olaudah Equiano, or Gustavus Vassa, the African*. New York: Negro Universities Press.

Escobar, Arturo (1995) *Encountering Development: The Making and Unmaking of the Third World*. Princeton, NJ: Princeton University Press.

Escott, Paul D., and David R. Goldfield, eds. (1991) *The South for New Southerners*. Chapel Hill: University of North Carolina Press.

Essed, Philomena (1991) *Understanding Everyday Racism: An Interdisciplinary Theory*. Newbury Park, CA: Sage Publications.

Fabian, Johannes (2007) *Memory against Culture: Arguments and Reminders*. Durham, NC: Duke University Press.

Fairbanks, Charles H. (1974) *The Kingsley Slave Cabins in Duval County, Florida, 1968*. Columbia: The South Carolina Institute of Archaeology and Anthropology.

Fanon, Frantz (1963) *The Wretched of the Earth*. New York: Ballantine Books.

——— (1967) *Black Skin, White Masks*. New York: Grove Press.

Fennell, Christopher C. (2010) Damaging detours: Routes, racism, and New Philadelphia. *Historical Archaeology* 44(1):138–54.

Ferguson, Leland (1992) *Uncommon Ground: Archaeology and Early African America, 1650–1800*. Washington, D.C.: Smithsonian Institution Press.

Fett, Sharla M. (2002) *Working Cures: Healing, Health, and Power on Southern Slave Plantations*. Chapel Hill: University of North Carolina Press.

Fields, Edda L. (2001) *Rice Farmers in the Rio Nunez Region: A Social History of Agricultural Technology and Identity in Coastal Guinea, ca. 2000 BCE to 1880 CE*. Ph.D. dissertation, history, University of Pennsylvania.

——— (2008) *Deep Roots: Rice Farmers in West Africa and the African Diaspora*. Bloomington: Indiana University Press.

Fikes, Kesha (2000) *Santiaguense Cape Verdean Women in Portugal: Labor Rights, Citizenship and Diasporic Transformation*. Ph.D. dissertation, anthropology, University of California Los Angeles.

Fikes, Kesha, and A. Lemon (2002) African presence in former Soviet spaces. *The Annual Review of Anthropology* 31:497–524.

Finkelman, P. (1996) *Slavery and the Founders: Race and Liberty in the Age of Jefferson*. Armonk, NY: M. E. Sharpe.

Finney, Nikky (1995) *Rice*. Toronto: Sister Vision: Black Women and Women of Colour Press.

Foner, Eric (1983) *Nothing but Freedom: Emancipation and Its Legacy*. Baton Rouge: Louisiana State University Press.

Foucault, Michel (1980 [1972]) *Power/Knowledge: Selected Interviews and Other Writings 1972–1977*. New York: Pantheon Books.

——— (1942) The negro family in Bahia, Brazil. *American Sociological Review* 7(4): 465–78.

Frazier, Franklin E. (1957 [1949]) *The Negro in the United States*. New York: MacMillan Company.

Fretwell, J. K. (1984) *Kingsley Beatty Gibbs and His Journal of 1840–1843*. St. Augustine, FL: St. Augustine Historical Society.

Froman, R. (1963) *Man and the Grasses*. Philadelphia: J. B. Lippincott Company.

Gaillard, M. (2000) Interview with the author, Mount Pleasant, South Carolina, June 28.

Gardner, David (2009) Plantation to power completes family tale. *The Daily Telegraph* (Australia), January 21, Z-Drop in 1:30 A.M. edition.

Gates, Henry Louis, Jr., ed. (1987) *The Classic Slave Narratives*. New York: Penguin Books.

Gay, Malcom (2008) A new life in New Philadelphia. *American Archaeology* 12(3): 26–31.

Geertz, Clifford (1973) *The Interpretation of Cultures*. New York: Basic Books.

Genovese, Eugene D. (1976 [1974]) *Roll, Jordan, Roll: The World the Slaves Made*. New York: Vintage Books.

Gibbs, George W. (1998) Videotaped interview with University of Florida ethnographic field team, National Park Service-sponsored Kingsley Heritage Celebration and Family Reunion, Fort George Island, Florida, October 10–11. On file at NPS Timucuan Preserve Office, Jacksonville, Florida.

Gibbs, Tyson (2006) *African Americans at Snee Farm Plantation, Mount Pleasant, South Carolina*. Atlanta: National Park Service, Southeast Region, Cultural Resources Division.

Gibbs, William Tucker (1998) Videotaped Interview with University of Florida Ethnographic Field Team, National Park Service sponsored Kingsley Heritage

Celebration and Family Reunion, Fort George Island, Florida, October 10–11. On file at NPS Timucuan Preserve Office, Jacksonville, Florida.

Gilroy, Paul (1991 [1987]) *There Ain't No Black in the Union Jack: The Cultural Politics of Race and Nation.* Chicago: University of Chicago Press.

―――― (1993a) *Small Acts: Thoughts on the Politics of Black Cultures.* London: Serpent's Tail.

―――― (1993b) *The Black Atlantic-Modernity and Double Consciousness,* 7th printing. Cambridge, MA: Harvard University Press.

―――― (1993c) It ain't where you're from, It's where you're at: The dialectics of diaspora identification. In *Small Acts: Thoughts on the Politics of Black Cultures,* pp. 120–45. London: Serpent's Tail.

―――― (2001 [2000]) *Against Race: Imagining Political Culture Beyond the Color Line.* Cambridge, MA: Harvard University Press.

Glissant, Édouard, and J. Michael Dash (1989) *Caribbean Discourse: Selected Essays.* Charlottesville: University Press of Virginia.

Glover, Faye L. (1970) *Zephaniah Kingsley: Nonconformist, Slave Trader, Patriarch.* Master's Thesis, Atlanta University, Atlanta, Georgia.

Goldfield, David R. (1982) *Cotton Fields and Skyscrapers: Southern City and Region, 1607–1980.* Baton Rouge: Louisiana State University Press.

Goode, Kenneth G. (1969) *From Africa to the United States and Then: A Concise Afro-American History.* Glenview, IL: Scott Foresman and Company.

Goodwine, Marquetta L., ed. (1998) *The Legacy of Ibo Landing: Gullah Roots of African American Culture.* Atlanta: Clarity Press.

Gould, Jeffrey L. (1998) *To Die in This Way: Nicaraguan Indians and the Myth of Mestizaje, 1880–1965.* Durham, NC: Duke University Press.

Gould, Virginia M., ed. (1998) *Chained to the Rock of Adversity: To Be Free, Black, & Female in the Old South.* Athens: The University of Georgia Press.

Graves, Joseph L., Jr. (2001) *The Emperor's New Clothes: Biological Theories of Race at the Millennium.* New Brunswick, NJ: Rutgers University Press.

Gray, Cecil L. (1933) *History of Agriculture in the Southern United States to 1860.* Washington, D.C.: Carnegie Institution of Washington.

Greene, Jack P., Rosemary Brana-Shute, and Randy J. Sparks, eds. (2001) *Money, Trade, and Power: The Evolution of Colonial South Carolina's Plantation Society.* Columbia: University of South Carolina.

Gregory, Steven (1998) *Black Corona: Race and the Politics of Place in an Urban Community.* Princeton, NJ: Princeton University Press.

Grime, William E. (1976) *Botany of Black Americans.* St. Clair Shore, MI: Scholarly Press.

Grist, D. H. (1986 [1953]) *Rice.* New York: Longman.

Gullah/Geechee Cultural Heritage Corridor Pre-Conference Tour (2010) Gullah-Geechee Cultural Heritage Corridor Commission document files, NPS Gullah/Geechee Cultural Heritage Corridor office, Sullivan's Island, South Carolina.

Guthrie, Patricia (1996) *Catching Sense: African American Communities on a South Carolina Sea Island.* Westport, CT: Bergin & Garvey.

Gutman, Herbert (1976) *The Black Family in Slavery and Freedom, 1750–1925.* New York: Pantheon Books.

Habersham, Richard (2000) Interview, Mount Pleasant, South Carolina, August 18.

Hacker, Andrew (1992) *Two Nations: Black and White, Separate, Hostile, Unequal.* New York: Ballantine Books.

Haley, Alex (1976) *Roots*. Garden City, NJ: Doubleday.

Haley, Alex, and David Stevens (1993) *Queen*. New York: W. Morrow.

Hall, D. (1962) Slaves and slavery in the British West Indies. *Social and Economic Studies* 11(4).

Hall, Stuart (1996) The after-life of Frantz Fanon; Why Fanon? Why now? Why black skin, white masks? In *The Fact of Blackness: Frantz Fanon and Visual Representation*. Alan Read, ed., pp. 12–37. Institute of Contemporary Art. Seattle: Bay Press.

Hamilton, Ruth Simms (1990) Toward a paradigm for African diaspora studies. In *Creating a Paradigm and Research Agenda for Comparative Studies of the Worldwide Dispersion of African Peoples*, Monograph No.1, Ruth Simms Hamilton, ed. East Lansing: Board of Trustees, Michigan State University.

Hamlin II, O. D. (2000) Interview, Mount Pleasant, South Carolina, June 15.

Hargrove, Thomas R. (1999) In search of Carolina gold: A genetic odyssey in rice— The journey of two Carolina sisters tells many stories. *Diversity* 15(3):24–26.

Harlan, Jack R., Jan M. J. De Wet, and Ann Stemler (1976) Plant domestication and indigenous African agriculture. In *Origins of African Plant Domestication*, Jack R. Harlan, Sol Tax, Jan M. J. De Wet, and Ann B. L. Stemler, eds., pp. 3–19. The Hague: Mouton Publishers.

Harris, David R. (1976) Traditional systems of plant food production and the origins of agriculture in West Africa. In *Origins of African Plant Domestication*, Jack R. Harlan, Sol Tax, Jan M. J. De Wet, and Ann B. L. Stemler, eds., pp. 311–56. The Hague: Mouton Publishers.

Harris, Jessica B. (1995) *The Welcome Table: African-American Heritage Cooking*. New York: Simon & Schuster.

——— (1998) *The Africa Cookbook: Tastes of a Continent*. New York: Simon & Schuster.

——— (1999 [1989]) *Iron Pots & Wooden Spoons: Africa's Gifts to New World Cooking*. New York: Simon & Shuster.

Harris, Joseph E., ed. (1993 [1982]) *Global Dimensions of the African Diaspora*. Washington, D. C.: Howard University Press.

——— (1996) The dynamics of the global African diaspora. In *The African Diaspora*, A. Jalloh and S. Maizlish, eds., pp. 7–21. College Station: Texas A&M University Press.

Harris, Marvin (1968) *The Rise*. New York: Columbia University Press.

Harrison, Ira E., and Faye V. Harrison, eds. (1999) Introduction: Anthropology, African Americans, and the emancipation of a subjugated knowledge. In *African American Pioneers in Anthropology*, pp. 1–36. Urbana: University of Illinois Press.

Heglar, Charles J. (2001) *Rethinking the Slave Narrative: Slave Marriage and the Narratives of Henry Bibb and William and Ellen Craft*. Westport, CT: Greenwood Press.

Helper, Hinton Rowan, and George Fitzhugh (1960) *Ante-Bellum: Three Classic Works on Slavery in the Old South*. New York: Capricorn.

Herbert, David, ed. (1985) *Heritage Tourism and Society*. New York: Wellington House.

Herrmann, Joachim (1989) World archaeology: The world's cultural heritage. In *Archaeological Heritage Management in the Modern World*, H. F. Cleere, ed., pp. 30–37. London: Unwin Hyman.

Herskovits, Melville J. (1937) The significance of the study of acculturation for anthropology. *American Anthropologist* 39:259–64.

––––– (1938) *Acculturation: The Study of Culture Contact*. New York: J. J. Augustin Publisher.

––––– (1958 [1941]) *The Myth of the Negro Past*. Boston: Beacon Press.

––––– (1965) *Acculturation: Cultural Dynamics*, pp. 159–81. New York: Alfred A. Knopf.

––––– (1968 [1928]) *The American Negro: A Study in Racial Crossing*. Bloomington: Indiana University Press.

Hess, Karen (1992) *The Carolina Rice Kitchen: The African Connection*. Columbia: University of South Carolina.

Heyward, D. C. (1993 [1937]) *Seed from Madagascar*. Columbia: University of South Carolina Press.

Hilliard, Sam B. (1978) *Antebellum Tidewater Rice Culture in South Carolina and Georgia*. Toronto: University of Toronto Press.

Hooker, R. J. (1981) *Food and Drink in America: A History*. Indianapolis: Bobbs-Merrill Company.

hooks, bell (1990) *Yearning: Race, Gender, and Cultural Politics*. Boston: South End Press.

House, Albert V., ed. (1954) *Planter Management and Capitalism in Ante-Bellum Georgia: The Journal of Hugh Fraser Grant, Ricegrower*. New York: Columbia University Press.

Howard, Peter (2003) *Heritage: Management, Interpretation, Identity*. London: Continuum International Publishing Group.

Howard, Rosalyn (2002) *Black Seminoles in the Bahamas*. Gainesville: University Press of Florida.

Hurston, Zora Neale (1979 [1928]) How it feels to be colored me. In *I Love Myself When I am Laughing*, Alice Walker, ed., pp. 151–55. New York: The Feminist Press, City University of New York.

Inikori, J. E., ed. (1982) *Forced Migration: The Impact of the Export Slave Trade on African Societies*. New York: Africana Publishing Company.

Inquai, Tebereh (1998) *A Taste of Africa: The African Cookbook*. Trenton, NJ: Africa World Press.

Israelsen, Orson W. (1958) *Irrigation Principles and Practices*. New York: John Wiley & Sons.

Jackson, Antoinette (2003) Africans at Snee Farm Plantation: Informing representations of plantation life at a National Historic Site. In *Signifying Serpents and Mardi Gras Runners: Representing Identity in Selected Souths*, Celeste Ray and Luke Eric Lassiter, eds., pp. 93–109. Athens: University of Georgia Press.

––––– (2004) *African Communities in Southeast Coastal Plantation Spaces in America*, Ph.D. dissertation, anthropology, Gainesville, University of Florida.

––––– (2008) Imagining Jehossee Island Rice Plantation today. *International Journal of Heritage Studies* 14(2):131–55.

––––– (2009) The Kingsley Plantation Community in Jacksonville, Florida: Transition and memory in a Southern American city. *CRM: The Journal of Heritage Stewardship* 6(1):23–33.

––––– (2010) Changing ideas about heritage and heritage resource management in historically segregated communities. *Transforming Anthropology* 18(1): 80–92.

Jackson, Antoinette (2011) Shattering slave life portrayals: Uncovering subjugated knowledge in U.S. plantation sites in South Carolina and Florida. *American Anthropologist* 113(3):448–62.

Jackson, Antoinette T., with Allan Burns (2006) *Ethnohistorical Study of the Kingsley Plantation Community.* Atlanta: National Park Service, Southeast Region, Cultural Resources Division.

Jackson, John L., Jr. (2001) *Harlem World: Doing Race and Class in Contemporary Black America.* Chicago: University of Chicago Press.

Jakes, John (1982) *North and South.* New York: Harcourt Brace Jovanovich.

Johns, Joe, and Justine Redman (2009) *Tracking Michelle Obama's Slave Roots.* CNN's AC 360, CNN.com, July 16, 2009.

Johnson, James Weldon (1933) *Along This Way: The Autobiography of James Weldon Johnson.* New York: Viking Press.

Johnson, Michael P., and James L. Roark, eds. (1984) *No Chariot Let Down: Charleston's Free People of Color on the Eve of the Civil War.* Chapel Hill: University of North Carolina Press.

Johnson, William (1993 [1951]) *William Johnson's Natchez: The Ante-Bellum Diary of a Free Negro.* Baton Rouge: Louisiana State University Press.

Johnston, Bruce F. (1958) *The Staple Food Economies of Western Tropical Africa.* Stanford, CA: Stanford University Press.

Jones, Norrece T., Jr. (1990) *Born a Child of Freedom, Yet a Slave: Mechanisms of Control and Strategies of Resistance in Antebellum South Carolina.* Hanover: University Press of New England.

Jones-Jackson, Patricia (1987) *When Roots Die: Endangered Traditions on the Sea Islands.* Athens: University of Georgia Press.

Joyner, C. W., ed. (1969) *In Search of a Black Past: Readings in Negro History.* New York: MSS Educational Publishing Company.

——— (1977) *Slave Folklife on the Waccamaw Neck: Antebellum Black Culture in the South Carolina Lowcountry,* dissertation, history, University of Pennsylvania.

Joyner, C. (1989) *Remember Me: Slave Life in Coastal Georgia.* Atlanta: Humanities Council.

——— (1999) *Shared Traditions: Southern History and Folk Culture.* Urbana: University of Illinois Press.

Kahn, Miriam (1996) Your place and mine: Sharing emotional landscapes in Wamira, Papua New Guinea. In *Senses of Place.* Steven Feld and Keith Basso, eds. Santa Fe, NM: School of American Research Press, pp.167–96.

——— (2000) Tahiti intertwined: Ancestral land, tourist postcard, and nuclear test site. *American Anthropologist* 102(1):7–26.

Kanneh, K. (1998) *African Identities: Race, Nation and Culture in Ethnography, Pan-Africanism and Black Literatures.* New York: Routledge.

Karp, Ivan, Christine Mullen Kreamer, and Steven D. Lavine, eds. (1992) *Museums and Communities.* Washington, D.C.: Smithsonian Institution Press.

Kawash, Samira (1997) *Dislocating the Color Line: Identity, Hybridity, and Singularity in African-American Narrative.* Stanford, CA: Stanford University Press.

Kellar, H. A., ed. (1936a) *Solon Robinson Pioneer and Agriculturist Selected Writings,* Volume I. Indianapolis: Indiana Historical Bureau.

——— (1936b) *Solon Robinson Pioneer and Agriculturist Selected Writings,* Volume II. Indianapolis: Indiana Historical Bureau.

Kelley, Robin D. G. (2002) *Freedom Dreams: The Black Radical Imagination*. Boston: Beacon Press.

Killion, Ronald, and Charles Waller, eds. (1973) *Slavery Time When I Was Chillun Down on Marster's Plantation*. Savannah: Beehive Press.

Kristiansen, Kristian (1989) Perspectives on the archaeological heritage: History and future. In *Archaeological Heritage Management in the Modern World*, H. F. Cleere, ed. London: Unwin Hyman.

Kup, A. P. (1975) *Sierra Leone: A Concise History*. Newton Abbot: David & Charles Limited.

Lachicotte, Alberta M. (1955) *Georgetown Rice Plantations*. Columbia, SC: The State Commercial Printing Co.

Lebrón, Manuel (1998) Transcript of videotape interview conducted by University of Florida graduate students for the National Park Service Kingsley Heritage Festival and Family Reunion, Fort George Island, Florida, October 10–11. On file at NPS Timucuan Preserve Office, Jacksonville, Florida.

——— (2005) *Seeking the Inner Zephaniah—A Descendant's Perspective*. http://manuellebron.blogspot.com/2005_10_01_archive.html, accessed December 9, 2010.

Lebrón, Sandra (1998) Transcript of videotape interview conducted by University of Florida graduate students for the National Park Service Kingsley Heritage Festival and Family Reunion, Fort George Island, Florida, October 10–11. On file at NPS Timucuan Preserve Office, Jacksonville, Florida.

Lee, Jeannette Gaillard (2000) Town of Mount Pleasant Document. www.townof-mountpleasant.com/DocumentCenter/Home/View/752, accessed January 5, 2012.

Lees, William B. (1980) Limerick, old and in the way: Archaeological investigations at Limerick Plantation. University of South Carolina, Institute of Archaeology and Anthropology, *Anthropological Studies 5*.

Lefebvre, Henri (1991 [1974]) *The Production of Space*, reprinted 2002. Oxford: Blackwell Publishing.

Lemelle, Sidney J., and Robin D. G. Kelly, eds. (1994) *Imagining Home: Class, Culture, and Nationalism in the African Diaspora*. London: Verso.

Leonard, Tom (2009) From the cotton fields to the White House: Genealogists trace Michelle Obama's roots back to six-year-old slave girl. *The Daily Telegraph* (London), October 8, 2009.

Leone, Mark P., and Parker B. Potter, eds. (1988) The recovery of meaning: Historical archaeology in the eastern United States. *Anthropological Society of Washington Series*. Washington, D.C.: Smithsonian Institution Press.

Lester, Julius (1968) *To Be a Slave*. New York: Dell Publishing Company.

Levine, Lawrence W. (1977) *Black Culture and Black Consciousness: Afro-American Folk Thought from Slavery to Freedom*. New York: Oxford University Press.

Lewicki, Tadeusz (1974) *West African Food in the Middle Ages*. London: Cambridge University Press.

Lewis, David L., ed. (1995) *W. E. B. Du Bois: A Reader*. New York: Henry Holt and Company.

Linares, Olga F. (1992) *Power, Prayer, and Production: The Jola of Casamance, Senegal*. Cambridge: Cambridge University Press.

Linder, S. C. (1995) *Historical Atlas of the Rice Plantations of the ACE River Basin: 1860*. South Carolina Department of Archives and History.

Little, K. L. (1951) *Mende of Sierra Leone: A West African People in Transition*. London: Routledge & Kegan Paul.

Littlefield, Daniel C. (1991 [1981]) *Rice and Slaves: Ethnicity and the Slave Trade in Colonial South Carolina*. Urbana: University of Illinois Press.

—— (1995) *Rice and the Making of South Carolina: An Introductory Essay*. Columbia: South Carolina Department of Archives and History.

Locke, Alain (1997) *The New Negro: Voices of the Harlem Renaissance*. New York: Touchstone, Simon & Schuster.

Lovejoy, Paul E. (2000) *Transformations in Slavery: A History of Slavery in Africa*. Cambridge: Cambridge University Press.

Lowenthal, David (1985) *The Past Is a Foreign Culture*. New York: Cambridge University Press.

—— (1996) *Possessed by the Past*. New York: The Free Press.

Lynd, Robert, and Helen Lynd (1929) *Middletown: A Study in Modern American Culture*. New York: Harcourt, Brace and Company.

Lyons, Mary E. (1997) *Catching the Fire: Philip Simmons, Blacksmith*. New York: Houghton Mifflin Company.

Maquet, Jacques (1972) *Civilizations of Black Africa*. New York: Oxford University Press.

Matory, J. Lorand (2005) *Black Atlantic Religion*. Princeton, NJ: Princeton University Press.

Mattoso, Katia M. deQueiros (1996) *To Be a Slave in Brazil 1500–1888*. New Brunswick, NJ: Rutgers University Press.

May, Philip S. (1945) Zephaniah Kingsley, nonconformist (1765–1843).*The Florida Historical Quarterly* 23(3):145–59.

Mbembe, Achille (2001) *On the Postcolony*. Berkeley and Los Angeles: University of California Press.

McCarthy, Kevin M. (1995) *Black Florida*. New York: Hippocrene Books.

McClaurin, Irma, ed. (2001) *Black Feminist Anthropology: Theory, Politics, Praxis, and Poetics*. New Brunswick, NJ: Rutgers University Press.

McDavid, Carol (2007) Beyond strategy and good intentions: Archaeology, race, and white privilege. In *Archaeology as a Tool of Civic Engagement*. Barbara J. Little and Paul A. Shackel, eds., pp. 67–88. Lanham, MD: AltaMira Press.

McIntosh, Roderick J. (1998) *Peoples of the Middle Niger: The Island of Gold*. Oxford: Blackwell Publishers.

McIntosh, Wm. Alex (1996) *Sociologies of Food and Nutrition*. New York: Plenum Press.

McKercher, Bob, and Hilary du Cros (2002) *Cultural Tourism—The Partnership between Tourism and Cultural Heritage Management*. Binghamton, NY: The Haworth Press.

McKissick, Floyd (1969) *Three-Fifths of a Man*. New York: Macmillan Company.

McKittrick, Katherine, and Clyde Adrian Woods (2007) *Black Geographies and the Politics of Place*. Toronto: Between the Lines.

Meltzer, Milton, ed. (1964) *In Their Own Words: A History of the American Negro 1619–1865*. New York: Thomas Y. Crowell Company.

Mercer, Kobena (1994) *Welcome to the Jungle: New Positions in Black Cultural Studies*. New York: Routledge.

—— (1996) Decolonisation and disappointment: Reading Fanon's sexual politics. In *The Fact of Blackness: Frantz Fanon and Visual Representation*, Alan Read, ed., pp. 114–31. Seattle: Bay Press.

Messer, Ellen (1989) Methods of studying determinants of food intake. In *Research Methods in Nutritional Anthropology*, Gretel H. Pelto, Pertti J. Pelto, and Ellen Messer, eds., pp. 1–33. Hong Kong: United Nations University.

Milanich, Jerald T. (1999 [1996]) *The Timuca*, Vol. I, *Peoples of America*. Oxford: Blackwell.

Miller, Floyd J., ed. (1970) *Blake or The Huts of America: A Novel by Martin R. Delany*. Boston: Beacon Press.

Miller, Randall M., and John David Smith, eds. (1998) *Dictionary of Afro-American Slavery*. New York: Greenwood Press.

Mintz, Sidney W. (1974) *Caribbean Transformations*. Baltimore: The John Hopkins University Press.

―――― (1986) *Sweetness and Power: The Place of Sugar in Modern History*. New York: Elisabeth Sifton Books and Penguin Books.

Mintz, Sidney W., and Richard Price (1992 [1976]) *The Birth of African-American Culture: An Anthropological Perspective*. Boston: Beacon Press.

Mitchell, Faith (1999) *Hoodoo Medicine: Gullah Herbal Remedies*. Columbia, SC: Summerhouse.

Mitchell, Margaret (1993 [1936]) *Gone with the Wind*. New York: Warner Books.

Mitchell, Patricia B. (1998) *Plantation Row: Slave Cabin Cooking—The Roots of Soul Food*. Chatham, VA: Patricia B. Mitchell at Sims-Mitchell House.

Mitchell, Patricia M. (1997 [1993]) *Soul on Rice: African Influences on American Cooking*. Chatham,VA: Patricia M. Mitchell at the Sims-Mitchell House.

Moorman, F. R., and W. J. Veldkamp (1978) Land and rice in Africa: Constraints and potentials. In *Rice in Africa*, I. W. Buddenhagen and G. J. Persley, eds., pp. 29–43. New York: Academic Press.

Morgan, Philip (1998) *Slave Counterpoint: Black Culture in Eighteenth Century Chesapeake and Lowcountry*. Chapel Hill: University of North Carolina Press.

Morris, Christopher (1995) *Becoming Southern*. New York: Oxford University Press.

Mount Pleasant Official Town Website (2000) *The History of Sweetgrass Baskets*, M. Jeannette Gaillard Lee, www.townofmountpleasant.com/DocumentView.aspx?DID = 751, accessed March 9, 2012.

Mudimbe, V. Y. (1988) *The Invention of Africa: Gnosis, Philosophy and the Order of Knowledge*. Bloomington: Indiana University Press.

―――― (1994) *The Idea of Africa*. Bloomington: Indiana University Press.

Mullin, Michael (1992) *Africa in America: Slave Acculturation and Resistance in the American South and the British Caribbean 1736–1831*. Urbana: University of Illinois Press.

Murray, Shailagh (2008) A family tree rooted in American soil: Michelle Obama learns about her slave ancestors, herself, and her country, October 2, 2008, *The Washington Post*.

National Park Service website (n.d.) Gullah/Geechee Cultural Heritage Corridor www.nps.gov/guge/index.htm, accessed December 10, 2010.

―――― (n.d.) Kingsley Heritage Celebration, www.nps.gov/timu/planyourvisit/khc_what_is_khc.htm, accessed December 9, 2010.

―――― Kingsley Heritage Celebration (2009) Press release, www.nps.gov/timu/planyourvisit/khc_pressrelease.htm, accessed December 9, 2010.

―――― Planning, Environment, & Public Comment (PEPC) database (n.d.) http://parkplanning.nps.gov/projectHome.cfm?projectID = 24119, accessed December 10, 2010.

National Register of Historic Places Nomination Form—Friendfield Plantation (1996) http://south-carolina-plantations.com/georgetown/friendfield-sampit-river.html#nr, accessed December 4, 2010.

National Research Council (1996) *Lost Crops of Africa*, Volume I: *Grains*. Washington, D.C.: National Academy Press.

Nelson, Nathaniel (2000) Interview, Mount Pleasant, South Carolina, June 24.

Netting, Robert M. (1986) *Cultural Ecology*. Long Grove, IL: Waveland Press.

Novack, George E. (1939) The challenge of the colonial plantation system. *The New International*, Volume V(12):343–45, December.

Ohnuki-Tierney, Emiko (1993) *Rice as Self: Japanese Identities through Time*. Princeton, NJ: Princeton University Press.

Okpewho, Isidore, Carole Boyce Davies, and Ali A. Mazrui, eds. (1999) *The African Diaspora: African Origins and New World Identities*. Bloomington: Indiana University Press.

Olmsted, Frederick Law (1959) *The Slave States*. New York: Capricorn Books.

——— (1971) *The Cotton Kingdom*. Indianapolis: Bobbs-Merrill Company.

Orser, Charles E., Jr., ed. (1996) *Images of the Recent Past: Readings in Historical Archaeology*. Walnut Creek, CA: AltaMira Press.

——— (1998) The Challenge of Race to American Historical Archaeology. *American Anthropologist*. 100(3):661–68.

——— (2004) *Race and Practice in Archaeological Interpretation*. Philadelphia: University of Pennsylvania Press.

——— (2007) *The Archaeology of Race and Racialization in Historic America: The American Experience in Archaeological Perspective*. Gainesville: University Press of Florida.

Otto, John S. (1989) *The Southern Frontiers, 1607–1860: The Agricultural Evolution of the Colonial and Antebellum South*. New York: Greenwood Press.

Painter, Nell Irvin (1997) *Sojourner Truth—A Life, a Symbol*. New York: W. W. Norton and Company.

Palmer, Rev. H. (2000) Interview, Mount Pleasant, South Carolina, June 29.

Paton, Diana, ed. (2001) *A Narrative of Events, Since the First of August, 1834, by James Williams, an Apprenticed Labourer in Jamaica*. Durham, NC: Duke University Press.

Patterson, Orlando (1982) *Slavery and Social Death: A Comparative Study*. Cambridge, MA: Harvard University Press.

——— (1991) *Freedom: Freedom in the Making of Western Culture*. New York: Basic Books.

——— (1998) *Rituals of Blood: Consequences of Slavery in Two American Centuries*. New York: Basic Civitas Books.

Patterson, Tiffany R., and Robin D. G. Kelly (2000) Unfinished migrations: Reflections on the African diaspora and the making of the modern world. *African Studies Review* 43(1):11–45.

Pearson, Edward A., ed. (1999) *Designs against Charleston: The Trial Record of the Denmark Vesey Slave Conspiracy of 1822*. Chapel Hill: University of North Carolina Press.

Pearson, James E. (1949) *The Carolina Rice Industry: A Study in Historical Geography*. Norman, OK: University of Oklahoma Press.

Perdue, Robert E. (1973) *The Negro in Savannah 1865–1900*. New York: Exposition Press.

Phillips, U. B. (1918) *American Negro Slavery*. New York: D. Appleton and Co.

—— (1946 [1929]) *Life and Labor in the Old South*. Boston: Little, Brown and Company.

Pollitzer, William S. (1999) *The Gullah People and Their African Heritage*. Athens: University Press of Georgia.

Pottier, Johan (1999) *Anthropology of Food: The Social Dynamics of Food Security*. Malden, MA: Blackwell Publishers.

Powell, William S. (1963) *The Proprietors of Carolina*. Raleigh, NC: The Carolina Charter Tercentenary Commission.

Pratt, Mary Louise (1992) *Imperial Eyes: Travel Writing and Transculturation*. New York: Routledge.

Pred, Allan, and Michael J. Watts (1992) *Reworking Modernity: Capitalisms and Symbolic Discontent*. New Brunswick, NJ: Rutgers University Press.

Price, Richard (1991) Subsistence on the plantation periphery: Crops, cooking, and labour among the eighteenth-century Surinam Maroons. In *The Slaves' Economy: Independent Production by Slaves in the Americas*. Ira Berlin and Philip D. Morgan, eds., pp. 107–27. London: Frank Cass & Co.

Pringle, Elizabeth A. (1994 [1913]) *A Woman Rice Planter*. Columbia: University of South Carolina Press.

Quinn, Charlotte A. (1972) *Mandingo Kingdoms of the Senegambia: Traditionalism, Islam, and European Expansion*. Evanston, IL: Northwestern University Press.

Raboteau, Albert J. (1980) *Slave Religion: The "Invisible Institution" in the Antebellum South*. Oxford: Oxford University Press.

Rappaport, Joanne (1990) *The Politics of Memory: Native Historical Interpretation in the Colombian Andes*. Cambridge: Cambridge University Press.

Rawick, George P., ed. (1972) *From Sundown to Sunup: The Making of the Black Community—The American Slave: A Composite Autobiography*. Westport, CT: Greenwood Publishing Company.

—— (1976a) *The American Slave: A Composite*. Westport, CT: Greenwood Publishing Company.

—— (1976b) *Florida Narratives—The American Slave: A Composite Autobiography*. Westport, CT: Greenwood Publishing Company.

Read, Alan, ed. (1996) *The Fact of Blackness: Frantz Fanon and Visual Representation*. Seattle: Bay Press.

Richards, Paul (1985) *Indigenous Agricultural Revolution*. Boulder, CO: Westview Press.

Rivers, Larry E. (2000) *Slavery in Florida: Territorial Days to Emancipation*. Gainesville: University Press of Florida.

Rodney, Walter (1982) *How Europe Underdeveloped Africa*. Washington, D.C.: Howard University Press.

Rogers, George C., Jr. (1970) *History of Georgetown County, South Carolina*. Columbia: University of South Carolina Press.

—— (1973) *A South Carolina Chronology 1497–1970*. Columbia: University of South Carolina Press.

—— (1980) *Charleston in the Age of the Pinckneys*. Columbia: University of South Carolina Press.

Romano, Renee (2006) *Race Mixing*. *Gainesville*: University Press of Florida.

Rosaldo, Renato (1989) *Culture & Truth*. Boston: Beacon Press.

Rosengarten, Dale (1994 [1986]) *Row Upon Row: Sea Grass Baskets of South Carolina Low Country*. Columbia: McKissick Museum University of South Carolina.

Ruffins, Fath Davis (1992) Mythos, memory, and history: African American preservation efforts, 1820–1990. In *Museums and Communities: The Politics of Public Culture*. Ivan Karp, Christine Mullen Kreamer, and Steven D. Lavine, eds., pp. 506–611. Washington, D.C.: Smithsonian Institution Press.

——— (2006) Revisiting the Old Plantation: Reparations, reconciliation, and museumizing American slavery. In *Museum Frictions: Public Cultures/Global Transformations*. Ivan Karp, Corinne A. Kratz, Lynn Szwaja, and Tomas Ybarra-Fraustora, eds., pp. 394–434. Durham, NC: Duke University Press.

Rymer, Russ (1998) *American Beach: A Saga of Race, Wealth, and Memory*. New York: HarperCollins Publishers.

Sawyer, Lena (2002) Routings: "Race," African diasporas, and Swedish belonging. *Transforming Anthropology* 11(1):13–35.

Sayers, Daniel O. (2007). Landscapes of alienation: An archaeological report of excursions in the Great Dismal Swamp. *Transforming Anthropology* 15(2):149–57.

Scarborough, William K. (1966) *The Overseer: Plantation Management in the Old South*. Baton Rouge: Louisiana State University Press.

Schafer, Daniel L. (1976) *Eartha M. M. White: The Early Years of a Jacksonville Humanitarian* (paper). Jacksonville: University of North Florida.

——— (1994) *Anna Kingsley*. St. Augustine, FL: St. Augustine Historical Society.

——— (1996) Shades of freedom: Anna Kingsley in Senegal, Florida, and Haiti. *Slavery and Abolition* 17(1):130–54.

——— (2000) Zephaniah Kingsley's Laurel Grove Plantation, 1803–1813. In *Colonial Plantations and Economy in Florida*, Jane G. Landers, ed., pp. 98–120. Gainesville: University of Florida Press.

——— (2003) *Anna Madgigine Jai Kingsley*. Gainesville: University Press of Florida.

Schwalm, Leslie A. (1997) *A Hard Fight for We: Women's Transition from Slavery to Freedom in South Carolina*. Urbana: University of Illinois Press.

Scott, David (1991) That event, this memory: Notes on the anthropology of African diasporas in the New World. *Diaspora* 1(3):261–84.

——— (1999) *Refashioning Futures: Criticism after Postcoloniality*. Princeton, NJ: Princeton University Press.

Scott, M. (2000) Interview, Mount Pleasant, South Carolina, August 17.

Searing, James F. (1993) *West African Slavery and Atlantic Commerce: The Senegal River Valley, 1700–1860*. Cambridge: Cambridge University Press.

Sells, William (1972 [1823]) *Remarks on the Condition of Slaves in the Island Jamaica*. Shannon: Irish University Press.

Seshadri-Crooks, K. (2000) *Desiring Whiteness: A Lacanian Analysis of Race*. New York: Routledge.

Shackel, Paul A. (2001) Public memory and the search for power in American historical archaeology. *American Anthropologist* 103(3):655–70.

Shackel, Paul A. (2003) *Memory in Black and White: Race, Commemoration, and the Post-Bellum Landscape*. Walnut Creek, CA: AltaMira Press.

——— (2011) *New Philadelphia: An Archaeology of Race in the Heartland*. Berkley and Los Angeles: University of California Press.

Shackel, Paul A., Paul A. Mullins, and Mark S. Warner, eds. (1998) *Annapolis Pasts: Historical Archaeology in Annapolis, Maryland*. Knoxville: The University of Tennessee Press.

Sharma, S. D., and William M. Steele (1978) Collection and conservation of existing rice species and varieties of Africa. In *Rice in Africa*, I. W. Buddenhagen and G. J. Persley, eds., pp. 61–67. New York: Academic Press.

Sheperd, Ruby (1939) Oral history conducted with Mrs. Elizabeth Dismukes. In *American Life Histories*, Federal Writers' Project Florida, 1936–1940.

Shepperson, George (1993) African diaspora: Concept and context. In *Global Dimensions of the African Diaspora*, 2nd ed., Joseph E. Harris, ed., pp. 41–49. Washington, D.C.: Howard University Press.

Singleton, Theresa A., ed. (1985) *Archaeology of Slavery and Plantation Life: Studies in Historical Archaeology*. Orlando, FL: Academic Press.

—— (1999) *"I, Too, Am America": Archaeological Studies of African-American Life*. Charlottesville: University Press of Virginia.

Singleton, Theresa A., and Mark Bograd (2000) Looking for the Colono in Colonware. In *Lines That Divide: Historical Archaeologies of Race, Class, and Gender*. James A. Delle, Stephen A. Mrozowski, and Robert Paynter, eds., pp. 3–21. Knoxville: The University of Tennessee Press.

Skinner, Elliott P. (1993) The dialectic between diasporas and homelands. In *Global Dimensions of the African Diaspora*, 2nd ed., Joseph E. Harris, ed., pp. 11–40. Washington, D.C.: Howard University Press.

Smalls, Joe (2000) Interview, Mount Pleasant, South Carolina, August 18.

Smart-Grosvenor, Vertamae (1992 [1972]) *Vibration Cooking or the Travel Notes of a Geechee Girl*. New York: Ballantine Books.

—— (1996) *Vertamae Cooks in the Americas' Family Kitchen*. San Francisco: KQED Books.

Smith, Alice R. Huger (1936) *A Carolina Rice Plantation of the Fifties*. New York: William Morrow and Company.

Smith, Julia Floyd (1973) *Slavery and Plantation Growth in Antebellum Florida 1821–1860*. Gainesville: University of Florida Press.

—— (1985) *Slavery and Rice Culture in Low Country Georgia 1750–1860*. Knoxville: University of Tennessee Press.

Smith, J. V. (1993) *The Jolas of Senegambia, West Africa: Ethnolinguistic Identity and Change across an International Border*, Ph.D. dissertation, University of Oregon.

Soja, Edward W. (1996) *Thirdspace: Journeys to Los Angeles and Other Real-and-Imagined Places*, reprinted 1998. Malden, MA: Blackwell Publishers.

Sollors, Werner (1997) *Neither Black nor White yet Both*. Cambridge, MA: Harvard University Press.

South Carolina Department of Natural Resources (2010) ACE Basin Project History. www.acebasin.net/history.html, accessed December 4, 2010.

Spanish Land Grants (1941) *Spanish Land Grants in Florida: Confirmed Claims*, Vol. IV. Tallahassee, FL: State Library Board.

Spivey, Diane M. (1999) *The Peppers, Cracklings, and Knots of Wool Cookbook: The Global Migration of African Cuisine*. Albany: State University of New York Press.

Stampp, Kenneth M. (1965) *The Era of Reconstruction 1865–1877*. New York:Vintage Books.

—— (1989 [1956]) *The Peculiar Institution: Slavery in the Ante-Bellum South*. New York: Vintage Books.

Stein, Maurice R. (1990 [1972]) *The Eclipse of Community: An Interpretation of American Studies*. Princeton, NJ: Princeton University Press.

Stephens, Jean B. (1978) *Zephaniah Kingsley and the Recaptured Africans*. El Escribano v15:71–76.

Stewart, Mart A. (1996) *What Nature Suffers to Groe: Life, Labor, and Landscape on the Georgia Coast, 1680–1920*. Athens: University of Georgia Press.

Stoler, Ann (1995) *Race and the Education of Desire*. Durham, NC: Duke University Press.

Stoney, Samuel G. (1964) *Plantations of the Carolina Low Country*. New York: Dover Publications.

Stowell, Daniel W., ed. (2000) *Balancing Evils Judiciously: The Proslavery Writings of Zephaniah Kingsley*. Gainesville: University Press of Florida.

Sudarkasa, Niara (1980) African and Afro-American family structure. *The Black Scholar* 11(8):37–60.

Suttles, Gerald D. (1973) *The Social Construction of Communities*. Chicago: University of Chicago Press.

Swanton, John R. (1969 [1946]) *The Indians of the Southeastern United States*. Grosse Pointe, MI: Scholarly Press.

Swarns, R., and Jodi Kantor (2009) First Lady's roots reveal slavery's tangled legacy. *The New York Times*, October 8, 2009.

Tademy, Lolita (2001) *Cane River*. New York: Warner Books.

Tannahill, Reay (1988 [1973]) *Food in History*. New York: Crown Publishers.

Tax, Sol, Jack R. Harlan, Jan M. J. De Wet, and Ann B. L. Stemler, eds. (1976) *Origins of African Plant Domestication*. The Hague: Mouton Publishers.

Thompson, Edgar T. (1975) *Plantation Societies, Race Relations, and the South: The Regimentation of Populations*. Durham, NC: Duke University Press.

Thompson, Paul (1978) *The Voice of the Past Oral History*. Oxford: Oxford University Press.

Thompson, Vincent B. (1987) *The Making of the African Diaspora in the Americas 1441–1900*. New York: Longman.

Thornton, John (1998 [1992]) *Africa and Africans in the Making of the Atlantic World, 1400–1800*. Cambridge: Cambridge University Press.

Timucuan Preserve/Kingsley Plantation news release dated October 25, 2010, www.nps.gov/timu/parknews/, accessed December 1, 2010.

Tölölyan, Khachig (1996) ReThinking diaspora(s): Stateless power in the transnational moment. *Diaspora* 5(1):3–36.

Tonkin, Elizabeth (1995) *Narrating Our Pasts: The Social Construction of Oral History*. Cambridge: Cambridge University Press.

Trinkley, Michael (2002) *Archaeological and Historical Investigations of Jehossee Island, Charleston County, South Carolina*. Columbia: Chicora Foundation.

Trouillot, Michel-Rolph (1995) *Silencing the Past: Power and the Production of History*. Boston: Beacon Press.

———— (1998) Culture on the edges: Creolization in the plantation context. *Plantation Society in the Americas* 5(1):8–28.

Tsunoda, Shigesaburo, ed. (1984) *Biology of Rice: Developments in Crop Science*. New York: Elsevier Science Publishing Company.

Turner, Lorenzo D. (2002 [1949]) *Africanisms in the Gullah Dialect*. Columbia: University of South Carolina Press.

Tuten, James H. (1992) *"Live and Die on Hobonny": The Rise, Decline, and Legacy of Rice Culture on Hobonny, 1733–1980*, Master's thesis, history, Winston-Salem, NC: Wake Forest University.

Underhill, Harry (1990) *Small Scale Irrigation in Africa in the Context of Rural Development*. Bedford, UK: Cranfield Press.

UNESCO (1972) Text of the Convention Concerning the Protection of World Cultural and Natural Heritage, www.unesco.org/, accessed March 22, 2011.

—— (2003) Text of the Convention for the Safeguarding of Intangible Cultural Heritage, www.unesco.org/culture/ich/index.php?lg = EN&pg = home, accessed March 22, 2011.

U.S. Census Bureau (1850) Slave Inhabitants in the Parish of St. Johns Colleton, South Carolina.

—— (1860) Slave Inhabitants in Jehossee Island, County of St. Johns Colleton, South Carolina.

—— (1870) Census Rolls, Duval County and St. Johns County, Florida.

—— (1908) *The First Census of the United States, 1790 South Carolina: Heads of Families*. Washington, D.C.: U.S. Government Printing Office.

—— (1920) Census Roll, Duval County, Florida.

—— (1990 [1864]) *The Eighth Census (1860): Population of the United States in 1860*. v. 1, reprint. New York: Norman Ross Publishing.

—— (2000) Census of the United States. Washington, D.C.: U.S. Government Printing Office.

U.S. Fish and Wildlife Services (August 2005) Ernest F. Hollings ACE Basin National Wildlife Refuge brochure, http://acebasin.fws.gov, accessed December 4, 2010.

—— (August 2007) Ernest F. Hollings ACE Basin National Wildlife Refuge website, http://acebasin.fws.gov, accessed December 4, 2010.

Uya, Okon Edet (1992 [1987]) *African Diaspora and the Black Experience in New World Slavery*. New Rochelle, NY: Third Press Publishers.

Uya, Okon Edet, ed. (1971) *Black Brotherhood: Afro-Americans and Africa*. Lexington: D.C. Heath and Company.

Valentine, David (2007) *Imagining Transgender: An Ethnography of a Category*. Durham, NC: Duke University Press.

Van Doren, M., ed. ([1955 [1928]) *Travels of William Bartram*. New York: Dover Publications.

Vernon, Amelia Wallace (1993) *African Americans at Mars Bluff, South Carolina*. Baton Rouge: Louisiana State University Press.

Vlach, Michael J. (1991) *By the Work of Their Hands: Studies in Afro-American Folklife*. Ann Arbor, MI: UMI Research Press.

—— (1993) *Back of the Big House: The Architecture of Plantation Slavery*. Chapel Hill: University of North Carolina Press.

Walker, Alice (1985) *The Color Purple*. New York: Pocket Books.

Walker, Karen J., ed. (1988) *Kingsley and His Slaves: Anthropological Interpretation and Evaluation*. Volumes in Historical Archaeology. Columbia: The South Carolina Institute of Archaeology and Anthropology.

Walker, Margaret (1966) *Jubilee*. Boston: Houghton Mifflin.

Walsh, Rebecca (2003) Global Diasporas: Introduction. *Interventions—International Journal of Postcolonial Studies* 5(1):1–11.

Walvin, James (2000) *Britain's Slave Empire*. Charleston: Tempus Publishing.

—— (2008) Slavery is still an election issue: Michelle Obama could be about to make a very American sort of history. *The Sunday Telegraph* (London), October 26, 2008.

Waring, Joseph I. (1970) *The First Voyage and Settlement at Charles Town 1670–1680*. Columbia: University of South Carolina Press.

White, Deborah G. (1985) *Ain't I a Woman? Female Slaves in the Plantation South*. New York: W. W. Norton & Company.

Whitten, David O. (1971) Antebellum sugar and rice plantations—Louisiana and South Carolina: A profitability study. *Economics*. New Orleans: Tulane University.

Wilkie, Laurie A. (1994) Ethnicity, community, and power: An archaeological study of the African-American experience at Oakley Plantation, Louisiana. *Archaeology/ Anthropology*, p. 436. UCLA.

—— (2001) Black sharecroppers and white frat boys. In *Archaeologies of the Contemporary Past*, V. Buchili and G. Lucas, eds., London: Routledge.

Williams, B. F. (1991) *Stains on My Name, War in My Veins: Guyana and the Politics of Cultural Struggle*. Durham, NC: Duke University Press.

Williams, D. (1995) *Them Dark Days: Slavery in the American Rice Swamps*. New York: Oxford University Press.

Williams, F. L. (1978) *A Founding Family: The Pinckneys of South Carolina*. New York: Harcourt Brace Jovanovich.

Williams, L. S. (1999) *Strangers in the Land of Paradise: The Creation of an African American Community, Buffalo, New York 1900–1940*. Bloomington: Indiana University Press.

Wolf, Eric R. (1997 [1982]) *Europe and the People without History*. Berkeley and Los Angeles: University of California Press.

Wood, B. (1995) *Women's Work, Men's Work: The Informal Slave Economics of Low-Country Georgia*. Athens: The University of Georgia Press.

Wood, Peter H. (1974) *Black Majority: Negroes in Colonial South Carolina from 1670 through the Stono Rebellion*. New York: W. W. Norton & Company.

—— (1976) Black labor-white rice: Colonial manpower and African agricultural skill in early Carolina. In *Shaping Southern Society: The Colonial Experience*. T. H. Breen, ed., pp.135–55. New York: Oxford University Press.

Woodward, C. Vann (1974) *The Strange Career of Jim Crow*. New York: Oxford University Press.

Wright, Donald R. (1990) *African Americans in the Colonial Era*. Arlington Heights, IL: Harlan Davidson.

Wright, Louis B. (1962) *The Cultural Life of the American Colonies 1607–1763*. New York: Harper Torchbooks.

INDEX

About the Author

Antoinette T. Jackson is an Associate Professor in the Department of Anthropology at the University of South Florida in Tampa. She received a Ph.D. in anthropology from the University of Florida, an M.B.A. from Xavier University in Cincinnati, Ohio, and a B.A. in Computer and Information Science from Ohio State University. She is also an All-American 100-meter hurdler, which she achieved as a student/athlete at Ohio State University. Before entering the academic field in 1998, Jackson pursued a career in the telecommunications industry and was employed as a product manager for AT&T/Lucent Technologies in Naperville, Illinois.

Jackson also directs the USF Heritage Research and Resource Management Lab, which she launched in 2006 as an avenue for community engagement and student participation in applied projects and initiatives with relevance outside the academic arena. The stated mission of the lab is preserving and promoting heritage as a key cultural resource through collaboration with communities and civic associations.

Jackson is interested in issues of identity and representation at public and/or national heritage sites. Her research focuses on heritage, heritage tourism, and the business of heritage research and resource management in the United States and the Caribbean. She has published in a wide range of venues, including *American Anthropologist* ("Shattering Slave Life Portrayals—Uncovering Subjugated Knowledge in U.S. Plantation Sites in South Carolina and Florida," Vol. 113, No. 3, pp. 448–62, 2011); *Transforming Anthropology* ("Changing Ideas about Heritage and Heritage Resource Management in Historically Segregated Communities," Vol. 18, No. 1, pp. 80–92, 2010); *CRM: The*

Journal of Heritage Stewardship ("The Kingsley Plantation Community in Jacksonville, Florida—Transition and Memory in a Southern American City," Vol. 6, No. 1, pp. 23–33, 2009); and *International Journal of Heritage Studies* ("Imagining Jehossee Island Rice Plantation Today," Vol. 14, No. 2, pp. 131–55, 2008). Additionally, Jackson is actively engaged in several research projects with the National Park Service including a federal appointment to a National Commission—the Gullah/Geechee Cultural Heritage Corridor Commission—in 2007 representing the State of Florida; the U.S.-Bahamian Underground Railroad Connection project; ethnographic research and research support in the community of Nicodemus, Kansas, for the Nicodemus National Historic Site; and the ethnohistorical study of the Jimmy Carter National Historic Site and its environs, including surrounding communities of Archery and Plains, Georgia. In 2010, Jackson interviewed former President Jimmy Carter as part of her research efforts. She looks forward to one day interviewing First Lady Michelle Obama as part of her ongoing research of postbellum plantation communities.

 green
press
INITIATIVE